Campbell Ogilvy at the Battle of Arbroath

By Robert Nock

Copyright © 2015 by Robert Nock

All rights reserved.

ISBN 978-1-62806-068-3 (paperback)

Library of Congress Control Number 2015946982

Published by Salt Water Media
29 Broad Street, Suite 104
Berlin, MD 21811
www.saltwatermedia.com

Cover Image via 99 Designs.
Interior illustration by Diana Mosteller

Please note that this is a work of historical fiction. While names, places, events, and other items may be true, their use as well as dialogue and such are products of the authors imagination. Any resemblence to real persons, living or dead, except as otherwise noted, is purely coincidental.

Prologue

"This way, lads," I yelled at the top of my voice as I led the way from the west gate of the abbey and onto the road to the Loan of the Leys. Our entire force retreated in an orderly fashion, with the men at the very back of our column keeping their swords and shields at the ready in case they needed to form a shield wall to fend off an attack from our rear. Although we had fought well, the tide of battle was favoring the Lindsays and I knew we had to take action to keep our retreat from turning into a slaughter...

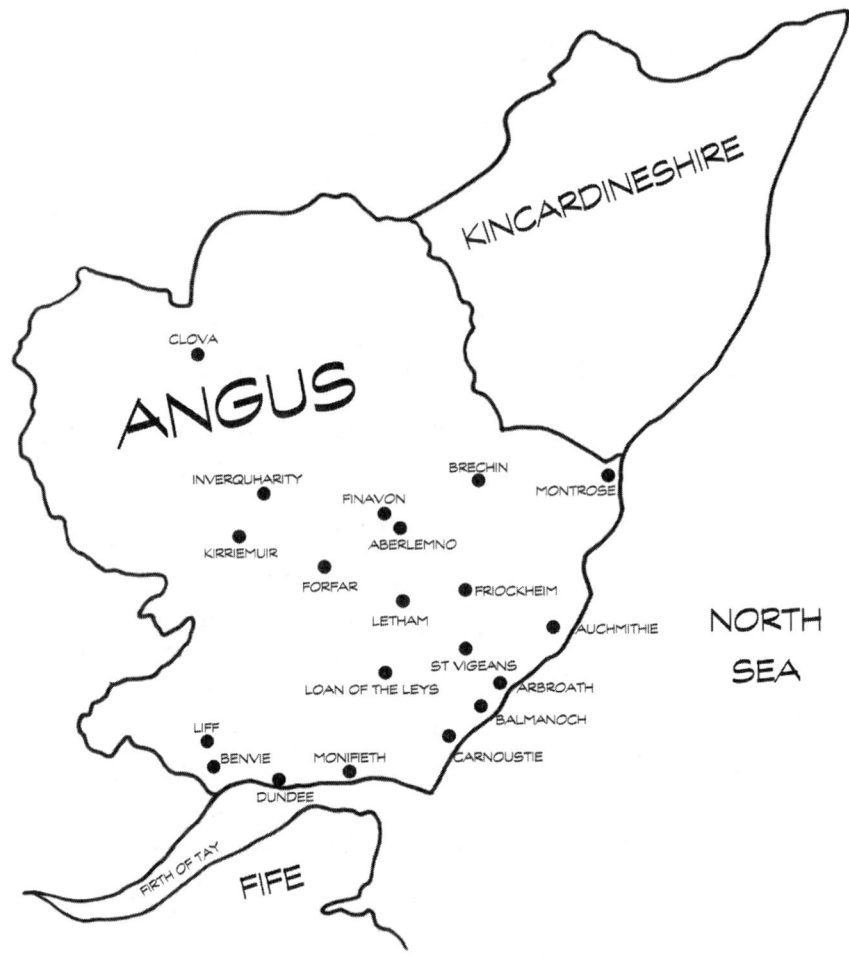

MAP OF ANGUS COUNTY

Glossary

'At – That
Abit – About
Afair – Before or afore
Ah – I
Alang – Along
Al'ays – Always
Alife - Alive
An' – And
Aroond – Around
Ata - At all
Awe or **A'** – All
Ay or **O'** – Of
Bade or **Bide** – Stay, to wait
Bark - news
Beak – Nose
Beest – Beast
Bestaw – Bestow
Blether – Nonsense talk
Bin – Been
Bit – But
Borin – Boring
Boss – The center of a shield. Usually made of brass or other metal and can be used as a weapon
Bother – Trouble
Braw – Good

Brigandine – Body armor. A leather or canvas garment lined with metal plates.
Burn – Creek or river
Cairn – Mound of rough stones
Cannae – Cannot
Cannie – Smart
Caparison – Cloth covering on a horse that provided protection and decoration
Caw – Occasion, passing visit
Claise – Close
Claymore – Scottish two-handed longsword
Close – Narrow alleyway
Coupon – A piece
Cudgel – Short staff or stick used as a club
Cuid – Could
Cuisse – Armor that protects the thigh
Dae – Do
Daein – Doing
Dain – Done
Destrier – Finest and strongest war horse. Bred and raised from a foal to be ridden in battle.
Dinna or **Dinnae** – Did not

Doctur – Doctor
Dornt – Don't
Driech – Cloudy, wet and rainy
E'en – Even
Evensong – Prayer service held in the late afternoon or early evening. Usually involved singing or chanting
Feuchin – Fought
Feuchin up – to deliver a sound beating
Fit – Healthy, capable
Fit like? – How are you?
Follaw – Follow
Foostie – Gone off
Foremaist – Foremost, First
Forenicht – Early part of the night, early evening
Frae – From
Frontispiece – elements that frame the main door to a building
Fur – For
Furraw – Furrow
Gain – Gone
Gang – Go
Gie – Give
Goad – Farming implement used to guide livestock
Greaves – Armor that protects the leg
Guid – Good

Haes – Has
Hangowre – Hangover
Hauns – Hands
Haur – Here
Hin' - Think
Hink – Think
Hoo – How
Hud – Had
Huir - Whore
Hulp – Help
Intae – Into
Jammy – Lucky
Jist – Just
Ken – Know
Kent – Knew
Kimmer - Young women
Lae - The rest, the remainder
Lik' – Like
Mah – My
Main – May
Mair – More
Mannie – Man
Memur – Remember
Michaelmas – Feast of Saint Michael. Usually celebrated on Sept 29th after the harvest is in.
Min' – Mind
Mist – Must
Mither – Mother
Mon - Man
Mony – Many

Mucky–Heap – A dirty, slatternly women or girl
Mukker – Friend
Na or Nae – No
Nam – Name
Nicht – Night
Noo – Now
O' - Of
Oan – On
Ofttimes – Often
Onie – Any
Oot – Out
Ourtright – Outright
Ower – Rather
Pat – Put
Puckle - Small amount
Puir – Poor
Rin – Run
Rite or Reit– Right
Sabaton – Armor that protects the foot
Sae – So
Secht – Sight
Scair – Score
Shogie–Bogie – Holding and rocking someone as you would put a baby to sleep
Shoods or **Shuid** – Should
Sodger – Soldier
Soond – Sound
Stoap – Stop
Stoatin – Great, exciting
Stone – unit of weight. One stone equals 14 pounds
Sussed – Figured
Swatch - Look
Tae – To
Teuk – Took
Th' – The
Thae – Those
Thare – There
Thin – Thing
Tis – Is
Tonsure (style or cut) – Hairstyle often worn by monks or priests where the top of the scalp has been shaved leaving a band of hair along the sides and back of the head.
Toon – Town
Top Coupon – Face, head
Twa – Two
Ur – Or
Urr – Are
Vera – Very
Villein – Serf, peasant farmer
Wance – Once
Wantae or **Wanttae** – Want to
Waur – Were
Wee – Little, short
Weel – Well
Weesht or Wheesht - Hush,

silence

Whin – When

Wi' – With

Wirk – Work

Witoot – Without

Wooldnt – Would not

Worthies - Notable persons within a particular social group or setting

Wull – Will

Ye – You

Yer – Your

Yett – Hinged gate, usually made of latticed wrought iron bars. Used as a defensive barrier for a castle and usually found only in Scotland

Yin – One

Chapter 1

"Campbell! Campbell!" My father's voice reverberated off the stone walls of the castle. "It's time for us to be going." I hurriedly pulled on my leather waistcoat and made sure my kilt was fitting properly and ran to meet my father.

Today was a special day, the harvest celebration of Michaelmas. My father was taking me into the town of Dundee for the festivities that were taking place. When I got outside my father was already mounted on Spirit, his favorite horse. Our servant, Thom, had my horse, Malice, ready for me and I quickly climbed into the saddle. My father smiled as I rode next to him. "Well done, son," he said approvingly. "You look like a true Scotsman. "

I couldn't help but flash a huge smile at my father's compliment. I had recently celebrated my 14th birthday. I was wearing the kilt outfit for the first time that I had received as my birthday gift. I was quite proud of my kilt. The Clan Ogilvy colors blended different shades of green together to make a very stylish tartan, one that I was proud to wear.

I remember that day very vividly. It was unusually warm for that time of year. The birds were singing and there was lots of sunshine under a bright blue sky as we rode towards Dundee. We passed recently harvested fields bordered by stone fences with yellow gorse bushes struggling to survive in the cracks and crevices of the stones. We passed woods where blue bells flowed over the forest floor in a beautiful carpet that covered the moss covered stumps and fallen limbs.

There was a lot of color at that time of year. Even the ponds and rivers we passed showed great patches of pink, blue and yellow as water mints, forget-me-nots and ragwort were flowering. It was a happy time.

Times hadn't been so happy recently. The plague had taken my sister, Davina, and my older brother Adair, the year before, leaving my parents with just myself and my younger sister, Fiona. Many of our tenant farmers had also suffered greatly during that time of pestilence, and the harvest had been very poor as a result.

The church we attended at that time had a priest who was a very fiery speaker. He told us the plague was Divine Retribution for all the sins we had committed. Every Sunday he would shout from the pulpit about the dangers of sin and temptation and how sickness and death awaited sinners. Father Greene, God rest his soul, was his name. He was a portly man with a red face that matched his fiery sermons. His hair, which was cut in the tonsure style, was completely white and was fuller on either side of his head than in the back. I remember how the tufts of white hair on the sides would bounce and shake when he became animated.

I have to admit, and may God forgive me for this, but I didn't like Father Greene very much. Even at that early age I doubted him when he said that sins caused people to become ill. I knew my brother committed lots of sins, but I never knew of any sins my sister committed.

One time after church, my father asked Father Greene why good people were being punished for their sins while others that had sinned far worse stayed healthy. Father Greene's reply was that, "God works in mysterious ways." I guess this is true because it wasn't long after this that the good Father himself came down with a high fever with lots of vomiting and loss of bowel control. He then began coughing up large quantities of blood and died. Maybe Father Greene sinned more than any of us were aware or maybe God does work in mysterious ways indeed.

Those troubles now seemed so far away on this bright late summer day as my Father and I rode side by side. As we neared the outskirts of town we passed a huge oak tree and a flock of sparrows perched in the tree began singing merrily. It was as if they were welcoming us.

Shortly after entering Dundee my father reined in his horse and turned to me, "Campbell, I have business to attend to in town.

I'll get something for us to eat and then you'll be on your own for a while. Be careful and stay on the main street. Don't go exploring any side streets, they can be dangerous."

"Aye, Father. I'll be careful," I replied. My parents had always been protective but had become even more so since the deaths of Adair and Davina.

Dundee was very crowded that day. We stabled our horses and set forth on foot to explore the town. It seemed every available foot of space along the main street was filled with merchants selling every imaginable food and merchandise. There were also jugglers and acrobats, performing myriad tricks and showing off their skills, hoping for a coin tossed their way. The streets were filled with what seemed the entire population of Angus. Rich and poor, young and old, they all seemed to be in town celebrating this special day.

We passed one stall that had the most delicious aromas emanating from an assortment of hot pies displayed on the counter. My father bought a venison pie and brought the steaming delicacy over to me. He divided it roughly into two parts and gave half to me and kept half for himself.

"I'm off to take care of my business now. Remember to be careful and stay out of trouble. I'll meet you back here when the church bell rings for evensong," my father said before he turned and walked away.

I was happy to be alone. I felt safe and grown-up walking through the streets of Dundee by myself. I was enjoying the venison pie and the hustle and bustle of the city. I quickly finished my pie and I found myself standing in front of an ale house that was on the corner of the main street and a smaller side street. The name of the ale house was The Crown. I remembered my older brother telling me about a street in Dundee, fronted by an ale house named The Crown that had as he put it, "Anything your heart might desire if you were willing to part with a silver coin or two."

I remembered my Father's warnings about being careful and staying away from side streets, but with so many people about I didn't think a short walk down this street would be of any harm. I didn't want to part with any silver coins but my 14-year-old curiosity was definitely peaked.

I had walked a short way down this street when I noticed the crowd here was different. There were no stalls selling goods and many of the people I passed seemed to be celebrating Michaelmas by ingesting large quantities of alcohol and engaging in different kinds of games of chance. The people here seemed poorly dressed compared to others in the main part of town. There were some well-dressed people but they were mostly older men in the company of much younger women.

As I turned to head back to the main part of town I became aware of movement on my right side and slightly behind me. My head suddenly exploded in a shower of bright light and I found myself flat on the ground with a searing pain on the right side of my head. Regaining my senses somewhat, I looked up to see three boys a few years my elder standing over me and looking down. The largest of the three had a sadistic sneer on his face and was holding a cudgel in his right hand that I realized was the source of the pain in my skull. I didn't realize it at the time but I had just met Alexander Lindsay, the future 4th Earl of Crawford. He also came to be known as the "Tiger Earl" and "Earl Beardie." He also became my mortal enemy.

"Get up, you snotnosed Ogilvy," Lindsay said.

I knew that if I stood up I would probably be knocked down again so I lay there and tried to think what to do. I was big for my age but the three of them were all older than me and at least my size so fighting them was out of the question. As I lay there I realized that my right hand, which was under my body, was resting on a rather good sized rock.

"Get up!" Lindsay screamed again and this time I made a motion as if to rise. A smile spread across my tormentors face as he prepared to use the cudgel on me again. I suddenly rolled over and flung my rock towards the sneering face and I had the satisfaction of seeing it strike him squarely in the mouth. The sneer turned to surprise and pain as he began to spit blood and broken teeth.

The other two boys were momentarily stunned at seeing their mate treated this way. I seized this moment to get up and hopefully make a getaway. "Get him!" my attacker screamed as I began to run. Unfortunately, the other two boys came to their senses and were able to grab me before I had gotten far.

I quickly found myself on the ground again, and this time all three boys began to kick me. I had no option other than to curl into a ball and hope I would survive what I knew would be a very savage beating. However to my surprise, after just a couple of kicks, I heard a voice yell "Stop!" and saw the side of a flashing blade smack solidly into the face of one of the boys. The boy that was hit let out a mournful cry of pain. All three of my attackers turned to see who was now attacking them. Standing with a sword raised above his head, ready to strike again, they saw a powerfully built man with the manner and weapons of someone accoustomed to fighting. The sword he had swatted my attacker with had a blade that was polished to a bright shine. The weapon looked especially deadly held in such a menacing manner as it reflected the afternoon sunlight. In addition to the raised sword he had a shorter sword hung from his left hip. He looked to be in his early 20's and he wore the attire of an upper class gentleman.

"Be gone!" the man shouted as he took a step towards the three, raising his sword even higher as he did so. With that, the three decided they had had enough. They quickly beat a hasty retreat, one clutching his mouth, another the side of his face.

"On your feet, lad," my rescuer said as he helped me to my feet. "Alexander Seton, at your service young Ogilvy. I don't believe we've met but I know your father and uncles well."

Although I had never met my benefactor before I had heard of him. He was a well born man whose family was well-known throughout Scotland. Alexander's father, who also had the given name of Alexander, had recently been knighted. I had also heard of the scandal caused when his father had his marriage to Alexander's mother annulled so he could marry Elizabeth Crichton. Elizabeth was the daughter of the Chancellor of Scotland and the annulment effectively disinherited Alexander.

"My name is Campbell Ogilvy," I introduced myself. "I thank you so very much, Mr. Seton. You saved me from a severe beating or worse."

"It was nothing, young Ogilvy, and please, my friends call me Sande," my rescuer said with a broad smile on his face. "I witnessed that whole incident from the time those three attacked you. I started to not interfere since you acquitted yourself very well at first but when all three were on you at one time I thought you might appreciate a hand."

"That I did and again I thank you. Do you know who they were? The one must have known me because he called me by my surname."

"Was nae bother, and the reason they knew you and attacked you is because you're wearing the Ogilvy Tartan. The boy who hit you was Alexander Lindsay. The Lindsays have never been big fans of your family," my rescuer explained. "David Lindsay is Alexander's father, and a more decent man you could never hope to meet. I'm afraid that young Lindsay is quite unlike his father. Are you in town alone?"

"No, my father came with me but he had some business to take care of in town. I'm supposed to meet him by the food stalls when the church bell rings for evensong."

"Well, it's about that time now, so how about if I walk with you till we find your father? I haven't seen your father in over a year and would like to see him again."

"That would be very nice sir but I have one other favor to ask of you," I said a bit hesitatingly.

"And what would that be?"

"Well, I promised my father I wouldn't go into the part of town I was in, and I was hoping you wouldn't tell him where you found me."

Sande gave a hearty laugh at this and said with a smile on his face, "Tell you what Campbell, if you won't tell anyone where I was I won't tell anyone where you were."

We both laughed and set off to find my father.

Chapter 2

My father was waiting for us when we came to the food stalls. He had a worried look on his face when we first saw him, but that changed to a look of concern when he saw my disheveled appearance. For all that I had been through, I really was not in bad shape. My new clothes did have some spots of dirt rubbed into the fabric, the left side of my face bore a bruise from the glancing blow of a boot, and of course the right side of my head was swollen and showing a bit of blood. All things considered, I think I was in much better shape than the fellow I hit with a rock or the other young man that had been hit with the side of Sande's sword.

Sande and I quickly explained what had happened, being careful to leave out the exact location of where I had been attacked. When told who the ringleader was, a look of anger crossed my father's face.

"Perhaps you should contact the local Justiciar and report this crime." Sande offered.

"I'm afraid that would not do much good," my father said. "I've just been to a meeting with Abbot Walter and other monks from the abbey in Arbroath. The meeting was to decide who will be the new Justiciar and they have chosen David Lindsay over my brother, Alexander. To make matters worse, this office has been bestowed not just on David himself, the current Earl of Crawford, but on whoever holds that title. That title will go to David's eldest son, Alexander Lindsay, upon David's death. To make matters even worse, the good Earl has indicated that he will transfer that title before his death when he feels his son is mature enough. That son is the man who attacked Campbell. It will be a dark day indeed when the biggest scoundrel in the county will be the one to dispense law and justice."

"Why was this position given to the Lindsays over us, Father?" I inquired. "I thought Abbot Walter had told Uncle Alexander he would be the next Justiciar?"

"The good abbot did say that to your Uncle Alexander. We Ogilvys even have a hereditary right to the position, but it appears that James Douglas, the clan chieftain of the House of Douglas, intervened," my father explained. "James told the monks that he wanted David Lindsay to be the Justiciar and the monks wanted to stay in the good graces of the most powerful family in the county of Angus. Unfortunately, Clan Douglas is nearly as powerful as King

James himself. Some say more powerful."

"Is most unfair," opined Sande.

"Life is unfair, but things have a way of working out in the end and I'm sure this will as well. Maybe in a few years Alexander Lindsay will be a better man than he is now. At any rate I thank you very much for helping my son. "

"Aye, was nae bother. In fact, I quite enjoyed giving those lads a much needed lesson in manners," Sande responded.

"It is still much appreciated. If my family can ever do anything for you, please don't hesitate to ask."

"Well sir, there is a matter I would like to discuss with you if I may?"

"Of course. What is it?"

"As you may be aware, my father had his marriage to my mother annulled so he could marry another woman."

"I had heard that," my father responded. "He married the daughter of our Chancellor, William Crichton, did he not?"

"He did," Sande continued, "and this annulment has caused me to be without lands or title. At some point, I will inherit my mother's lands and the title that goes with them. Until then I have been supporting myself through service to the Crown. The past few years I have served in the common army of King James as a man-at-arms. However, now that we are at peace, I have been released from my military duties and am in need of employment. I was hoping you or your brother might have a position available that I would be suited for."

"Has your father cut you off completely?"

"No, he has offered to provide me with any funds I need but I don't want his charity. If he feels I am no longer his son, then he can keep his money."

"Your feelings are understandable." Changing the subject my father asked, "What type of weaponry are you familiar with?"

"I've been well trained in all types of weapons," Sande replied. "I'm well versed with the sword, spear, axe and mace. I'm even proficient with the longbow and crossbow. I've also had experience at training others. I could teach young Campbell here the skills of a warrior along with anyone else you might want trained. In addition to my military training, I also have knowledge of farming, and I am experienced with the caring and raising of farm animals. I feel I could be an asset to you and your brother."

I was quite excited at Sande's offer. The thought of being trained in the proper way to use the implements of war was irresistible to my young ears. I began to imagine myself in a dazzling suit of armor leading a charge of like-clad knights astride a ferocious destrier against an enemy of our King.

"I'm sure we have a position available that you would be well suited for," I heard my father say, which shook me out of my reverie. "I'll need to talk with my brother about that, but in the meantime I insist you stay with us."

"That is most generous of you, Mr. Ogilvy, but I couldn't impose on you that way."

"Nonsense, it will be an honor having you as a guest. I will be offended if you don't accept my offer."

"Well, in that case, if you're sure its nae bother I gratefully accept your offer and thank you very much."

"It's nae bother at all. It will be our pleasure to have you as a guest."

"In that case, I'll take care of some business I have in town and then ride directly to your lands. It's Inverquharity Castle, is it not?"

"It is. Do you know how to get there?"

"Aye, that I do."

"Well then, thank you again for helping my son. We will look forward to seeing you in a wee while."

Sande bowed and we took our leave of one another. My father and I began our walk back to where we had stabled our horses. We hadn't gone far when we ran into my Uncle Alexander.

My father was a tall man, over six feet. He was about two inches taller than my uncle who, although shorter, was a bit heavier. My uncle was also the oldest male of the family and hence had inherited the lands and title that went with it.

"Hello, Campbell," my uncle greeted me. "You look like you've been in a fight."

"Indeed he has," replied my father. "With none other than the future Justiciar of Angus himself, Alexander Lindsay, and his friends. Although I think my lad, along with some help from his friend Alexander Seton, gave a bit more than he took."

"Damn Lindsays!" exclaimed my uncle, as his face began to turn red as it often did when he got angry. "I guarantee the good monks of the abbey will come to regret their action this day, making the Master of Crawford their chief Justiciar." Taking a deep breath to calm himself, my uncle turned to me with a smile on his face and said, "Tell me what happened, Campbell, and don't leave out any details, especially not the parts about how you gave the Lindsay gang a proper feuchin up."

I smiled and proudly related the details of my adventure, especially the part about subduing my adversary with the rock. After I was finished, my father told my uncle about Sande's experience and his request for a position at Inverquharity.

"What do you think about bringing young Seton on to train Campbell and maybe a few others as well?"

"Alexander Seton, eh?" my uncle responded with a thoughtful look on his face. "That's the one who was treated so badly by his father, isn't he? Went from an aristocrat to a bastard overnight."

"Aye, that's the one. However he evidently knows his stuff and comports himself well like a true gentlemen."

"If you like him, that's good enough for me. He sounds like someone who would be an asset to us," my uncle replied, having quickly made up his mind. "We've been a bit negligent in providing training in the martial arts at Inverquharity. I don't mind admitting that this business of Lindsay being our new Justiciar makes me more than a bit nervous. In these lawless days being able to handle the implements of war will be a tremendous asset. With the appointment of the Master of Crawford as the new Justiciar, things will only become more lawless. I think we should make that training available to any local free man who wants it. Having a band of trained men available might be a good thing to have at hand, especially now with Lindsay being the law."

"I agree with those sentiments exactly, Alexander," said my father. "I think Mr. Seton will be a tremendous asset to us. Not only because of his experience with the implements of war but also because of who is father is. I know the relationship between Sande and his father might be a bit strained right now but I'm sure in an emergency the elder Seton would come to his son's aid. With Sande being aligned with us that aid would be to our benefit as well. Turning to me, my father asked, "What do you think, Campbell, do you want to learn to be a warrior?"

"Aye, very much so," I replied with a big smile on my face.

"In that case, since it's late, let's head for home," my father said. "We should be there when Sande arrives and you need to explain to your mother how you got your new clothes messed up."

With that we started on the long ride back to Inverquharity. We were able to get there shortly after dark. Sande arrived about an hour later. We had to repeat the day's events to my mother and Fiona as well as Thom and his wife, Besse, who was our cook. To my great relief, my mum was not at all concerned about the damage to my clothing. The minor injuries to my face concerned her much more. She insisted on applying a poultice to the injury on the side of my head that had been caused by the blow from Lindsay's cudgel.

Sande was very well received by everyone. We all enjoyed his stories of military service to the King. He even told us a little about the problems he had suffered as a result of the annulment of his parents' marriage. It was obvious that was a sore subject for him so no one questioned him further. I couldn't help notice that Fiona was especially fascinated with our visitor.

After we had told and retold the day's events, we sat down to a hot meal served by Besse. We all ate our fill. Then the four of us, my father and I along with Uncle Alexander and Sande sat around the fireplace in our great hall. We drank ale and nibbled on a plate of cheese that Besse had set out for us as we talked with Sande about his new position at Inverquharity.

"We can use your help with overseeing some of the work on the farm but the main thing we hope you do is teach Campbell along with some others the art of warfare," my uncle stated.

"I would be more than happy to do that," Sande replied. "I think young Campbell has the makings of a fine warrior."

I wasn't sure if Sande was serious or just being nice. Either way I liked hearing his compliment. I couldn't help but have the fantasy again of leading a charge against a formidable foe.

"I can start the training in the morning if that is agreeable with everyone," Sande continued.

"That would be grand," my uncle replied as he drained the last of his ale and stood up. "Let's get an early start tomorrow. The sooner we begin, the sooner we'll have Campbell ready to defend Inverquharity against any and all enemies. I'm off to bed now. I'll see you all bright and early in the morning."

We then retired for the evening. With the unfortunate losses we had suffered from the plague we had a number of spare bed chambers and were able to provide Sande with a private chamber on the second floor. My family had our quarters in the wing off the main part of the castle. The third floor of the Castle is where Uncle Alexander, his wife, Janet, and their toddler son, Alex, had their chambers.

I didn't think I would be able to sleep with the day's events still going through my mind and my excitement about my upcoming training. However, as soon as I lay down I was sound asleep, and didn't stir until the first rays of morning began to brighten my chamber.

Chapter 3

I was the first one up the next morning. I quickly dressed, drew a bucket of water from the well on the first floor and used that to wash my face and clean my teeth. I hurriedly wolfed down some cold mutton stew that was still in the iron kettle that was dangling over the now cold ashes in the kitchen fireplace. It was cool and misty when I walked outside, but the sun was beginning to break through. I sat down on a tree stump to await Sande.

I didn't have long to wait, for in just a few minutes I was startled to hear Sande's voice behind me saying, "Hello, Campbell, are you ready to start?"

"Aye, that I am," I replied getting to my feet.

"Then let's begin," Sande said as he walked over to a grassy area a few feet from the castle, motioning me to follow him. Once on the grassy area, Sande handed me one of two wooden swords he had been carrying and my training began.

Sande turned out to be an excellent trainer. He made it easy for me to learn how to handle the instruments of war. That first session we started training with the wooden swords and some wooden poles in place of spears. Sande began by showing me a few basic moves of how to thrust, parry and block with a sword and how to stab, slash and throw with a spear.

That first day we trained until late morning. After our noon day meal, I spent the rest of the day doing chores around the castle. We followed that same procedure almost every day. Usually in the afternoons Sande accompanied me on my rounds around the castle. Although he was a few years older and my teacher, Sande and I became close friends. More like brothers, in fact, than friends.

I had been training with Sande for a fortnight when one afternoon Uncle Alexander asked me to drive the wagon into Forfar to pick up some supplies from a local merchant. The supplies were valuable enough that my uncle didn't want to send just the farmhands after them. I agreed to go along to keep an eye on things.

I took two helpers with me and we made good time getting into town. The merchant was expecting us and we quickly loaded the wagon. I paid for the supplies with the silver coins my uncle had given me. As I left the merchants shop, I headed for the wagon, and to my shock and surprise, I nearly ran head on into none other than Alexander Lindsay in the company of his father.

Lindsay was as surprised to see me as I was to see him. However, he recovered quickly and with an evil sneer on his face said, "Well, well, if it isn't the little shite from Dundee and without his protector." I wasn't armed but Lindsay was, and as he spoke, he reached for the sword hanging at his side.

There is no question in my mind that Lindsay would have killed me on the spot had his father not been there. However, David Lindsay quickly intervened by shouting, "Leave it be!" as he grabbed his son roughly by the shoulder and pulled him away. Lindsay took his hand off his sword but he continued to glower at me as they walked away.

As they moved off, I had the satisfaction of seeing the source of a lot of Lindsay's anger towards me. A large ugly scar extended from Lindsay's left upper lip down diagonally through the lower lip and onto his right chin. The rock I had struck him with had done more damage than I realized and the scar it left would be a permanent reminder of our encounter. I also noticed that Lindsay had started to grow a beard in an attempt to conceal the damage.

Walking back to the wagon, I noticed I was breathing hard and shaking a bit from my close call. The two helpers I had with me hadn't even noticed what had happened and I saw no reason to tell them. I just climbed into the wagon, slapped the reins lightly on the backs of our two horses, and started on the trip back to Inverquharity. I didn't calm down completely until we were nearly home.

One good thing that came out of the encounter with Lindsay is that it impressed upon me the importance of learning how to use the weapons of war. It was evident with the likes of Lindsay around

I would need that training and I would probably need it sooner rather than later.

I trained in earnest from that day forward. Even Sande noticed a new determination in how I approached my lessons. The more I learned, the more I realized I needed to learn. I was fortunate to have such a good teacher as Sande. Even though we were friends he didn't let that stop him from being tough with me when he needed to be. On more than one occasion, when I didn't block one of Sande's sword thrusts properly he would ram the tip of the wooden sword into my belly hard enough to knock the wind out of me.

"If you block that poorly in battle, wee laddie, it will be your last battle," Sande told me a number of times as he would help me to my feet.

I was amazed at the large number of moves that could be made with a sword, more than 150 of them, and Sande expected me to master them all. I was taught how to handle a shield to provide myself with maximum protection and how to use the heavy boss as well as the edge of the shield as an offensive weapon. I learned how to pull the enemy's shield down with the edge of an axe and follow through with a killing sword thrust to the enemy's now exposed head and chest. I was given lessons in how to use maces and flails; spears and poleaxes; and the longbow.

The longbow was probably the most difficult weapon for me to master and in truth I never really did master it completely. The huge bow made out of wood from the Yew tree took all my strength just to pull the bow string all the way back let alone aim it correctly.

I eventually managed to use even that weapon with a reasonable degree of proficiency.

Often, Uncle Alexander and my father would watch us train. On those days I tried extra hard to execute the moves Sande had taught me with precision and accuracy.

On one particular day, a couple of weeks into my training, my father and uncle approached us in the company of three other men. One of the men I recognized as a friend I had known for many years. His name was James MacGelland. He was the son of the Earl of Boece, and we had known each other since we were wee.

The other two men I didn't recognize. It turned out they were from farms not far from Inverquharity. One fellow was a huge lad who had been raised in the highlands. His name was Duncan Overton and his family farmed as freemen on land that bordered Inverquharity. He was over six feet tall with massive arms as large as small tree trunks. He had blond hair that he wore long. He had a pleasant disposition, though I found out later he could get quite angry if something was bothering him.

The other young man was named Malcome Stoylle. He was also a farmer's son. It turned out his father was from the same area of the Highlands where Duncan had been raised. Malcome was also a big lad, although not as big as Duncan. He had dark hair and seemed to always have a smile on his face. Both Malcome and Duncan had the heaviest brogues I had ever heard.

After introductions were made, my uncle informed us that the three newcomers were joining us on a permanent basis. He told us they were the first members of a defense force that my uncle was raising to protect Inverquharity and the surrounding area against any lawless elements. Those lawless elements we all knew to be Alexander Lindsay and his cohorts.

"I want everyone to know," my uncle said, "that we're raising this force with the full knowledge and support of our King James. In fact, our king has even given us a license to install an iron yett to protect the main part of Inverquharity castle from intruders."

I was impressed and surprised that the King would allow any of his subjects to raise what amounted to a private army, let alone install a yett to protect their castle. Giving someone a license to install a yett and to allow them to raise their own defense force was an unusual accommodation and honor bestowed on only the most trusted subjects. It was also proof that even the Crown was becoming worried about the power of Clan Douglas and its supporters.

Our small group had now grown to five. After that first mornings practice the five of us sat together sharing a noon time meal prepared by Besse and drinking some of her fresh made ale. Before long the conversation turned to each of our reasons for agreeing to receive the training.

"What made you sign up for this?" my friend James asked me.

"For probably the same reasons you have," I replied. "I've always wanted to learn the ways of a warrior and it's a bit of an adventure. Isn't that why you've signed up?"

"Not hardly," James said with a laugh. "It appears that a number of the lovely lasses I've been seeing back home have conceived a wee one. Our local Justiciar thought it best if I left town for a while and my father, who is tired of paying damages, agreed with him, so here I am."

We all laughed at James' answer. I had forgotten that James, who was a couple of years my senior, had the reputation of being a bit of a rake.

"And why did you two join?" I asked Duncan and Malcome.

"Fur a dinnae lik' farming. Mah faither n' grandfather love that wirk bit tis nae fur me," Duncan responded with a heavy Highland brogue.

"Ah think thes trainin' will enable me tae someday serve th' king an' Scootlund in th' common army. Ah also want tae dae somethin' different, farmin' is a bit borin,'" said Malcome in a brogue as heavy as Duncan's.

"An' a' wantae learn howfur tae uise a sword n' spear. I'v al'ays thought th' lif o' a fighter mist be an stoatin' adventure," Duncan added.

After we finished our dinner, I went out to do my afternoon chores. Sande agreed to share his bed chamber with James until other accommodations could be found and the two of them went to set up a cot and get James moved in. Duncan and Malcome lived close enough so they could ride in each morning for their training and still be home in the early afternoon to help out with their families farming activities.

The time passed quickly. The days turned into weeks and the weeks into months. Before I knew it a full year had passed. During that year, Uncle Alexander had recruited more men to our training group. Some of those men were volunteers that just wanted the training along with a place to stay and the meals that my uncle provided. However, most were paid a salary under a contract that obligated them to render aid to Uncle Alexander in an emergency.

Our group had now grown to 27 young men, although that figure would vary from month to month. Whenever Sande deemed someone to be proficient in the weapons of war he would release them from active training with the understanding they would rejoin our group whenever the need arose. Some of these men were the sons of our peasant farmers but most came from other farms and villages, many from as far away as Arbroath.

By this time I had mastered many of the weapons and was even beginning to instruct some of the newer members of our group. We were also fortunate that a man joined us that had served with Sande in the common army. He had fought with him in some of the border skirmishes against the English. Philip Alansoun was from the highlands. He was older than the rest of us, nearly 30 years of age. He was short and wiry. However, what Philip lacked in size, he more than made up for in skills and demeanor. On the right side of his face, he sported an ugly red scar that ran from the top of his cheek nearly to his chin. He had piercing blue eyes, and over the left eye, he had a scar on his forehead that extended onto the cheek below. His lips were thin and they seemed to be set in a perpetual scowl. I don't think you could ever face a more menacing person on a battlefield than Philip Alansoun.

Philip taught us how to fight as a group. He taught us to stay together when attacking as well as when we were being attacked and to fight as a single unit at all times. He showed us how to overlap our shields in formation so each person's shield not only protected the person holding the shield, but gave some protection to the men on either side of them as well.

He also taught us the finer points of warfare as well as the psychological aspects of battle. Philip explained, in his highland drawl, that in battle "Ofttimes tis better tae gie a mon a serious wound ower than killing him ourtright. Whin ye kill a mon ourtright ye tak' yin body oot o' th' battle, bit if ye wound yin ye tak' that body oot n' a' yin or twa o' his mukkers that wull stoap tae hulp him."

We stuck to our schedule of training in the mornings with the afternoons free for any other labors our lads may have needed to address. We did this pretty much year round except for a few weeks in the planting season, harvest time, and over Christmas.

I quite enjoyed the training and enjoyed training others even more. By the time my 16th birthday came near, I was training others full time. Most of our trainees had now graduated to using actual swords and weapons instead of the wooden ones and the clang of metal hitting metal could be heard from early morning to noontime at Inverquharity most every day except Sundays.

I used an old rusted claymore that belonged to my father. The others had similar weapons they got from their fathers or were able to borrow from friends. Only Sande and Philip along with one or two of the others, that came from well to do families, had proper weapons.

Even older weapons, though not in the best repair, could still inflict serious injury if not used properly or used in a careless fashion. We had to be careful not to kill one another in training and we did a good job of that. We did have some mishaps that produced our share of cuts and bruises. There was even one broken arm, but no one was seriously hurt.

The large number of people now training at Inverquharity was beginning to interfere with the farming activities at the castle. One day Uncle Alexander called Sande and I together and told us, "Lads, as you may have noticed we're getting cramped for space here at Inverquharity. To remedy that situation I sent an emissary to King James to inform him of our predicament. Our good King, through his regent, Sir Alexander Livingston, has granted us the use of the old Balmanoch Farm. When the previous owner died several years ago he was in arrears on the taxes and so ownership has reverted to the Crown. The castle that was there is now in ruins but there's a large stone barn with a good slate roof that will be ideal for taking meals and sleeping. The woods there are teaming with game and there are lots of fallow fields that will be ideal for training. It's only two miles from Arbroath which will make things easier for the lads that come from that area. If there are no objections I'd like to move all our training there as soon as possible."

"I think that's a good idea," replied Sande. "Today is Thursday, I don't see any reason why we couldn't move there Monday morning."

"Is Monday good with you, Campbell?" my uncle asked.

"Braw with me," I answered.

"Then it's settled. First thing Monday morning we'll move our training to Balmanoch farm."

I was very much in favor of moving our training to Balmanoch. The majority of our trainees were from the Arbroath area and this meant that more people could attend our morning sessions but still live with their families. There was also more available space for our training and the large barn would provide better accommodations for those that needed a place to stay. As beneficial as this move was for us, it turned out to be even more beneficial to the town of Arbroath and its citizens. In fact, it provided protection to the town during a traumatic event that would have resulted in far more damage and many more deaths than it did, if we had not been at Balmanoch.

Chapter 4

Early Monday morning saw a flurry of activity at Inverquharity as we prepared to move our training to Balmanoch. Wagons were hitched to horses in order to carry cots, cookware, extra weapons, and other items we would need at our new location.

It was in the midst of this activity that my father approached me riding Spirit. He was holding the reins to Malice, who was saddled and trailing behind them. "Campbell, I need you to accompany me on a trip into Forfar. There are plenty of helping hands here so you won't be needed for the move."

I didn't want to leave but I could tell my father had something important for us to do. "Aye, I'll just tell Sande I'm leaving."

"Not necessary. I've already explained things to Sande. Hop on," my father responded as he motioned for me to get on my horse.

I quickly climbed aboard Malice and my father and I began the short ride to Forfar.

"What's this trip all about?" I asked as we coaxed our horses into a brisk trot.

"You'll find out soon enough," my father replied with a smile on his face.

Although I was reassured by my father's smile that nothing bad was happening my curiosity was definitely piqued. A couple more attempts to glean some information from my father about our trip were met with the same smile and evasive answer. I realized that whatever surprise my father had in store for me would have to remain just that for the time being.

I settled back in the saddle to enjoy the pleasant ride into Forfar. It wasn't long before we were in the town and my father stopped his horse in front of the swordsmith's shop and dismounted. I did the same. As I did, I could hear the banging and clanging of iron and steel being shaped that was emanating from inside the shop.

"Well, Campbell, have you figured out why we're here?"

"I have no idea," I replied, now truly perplexed.

"Well, you're doing a fine job with your training and you're getting older. I thought it was high time to get you a proper sword so that you wouldn't have to make do with my rusty hand-me-downs."

I could scarcely believe my ears. I was amazed that I was getting a sword at all, let alone a sword made by this particular swordsmith. George Wilkinson was probably the best sword maker in all of Angus, if not in all of Scotland.

"Come inside," my father said as he turned and led the way inside the shop.

The interior of the shop was hot and smoky. My eyes watered a bit as I strained to see through the coal smoke that filled the interior of the shop. In the back was a large man covered in perspiration who was banging away at an object on his anvil. Hearing us enter his shop he carefully lowered what he was working on into a bucket of water. Thick clouds of steam rose up as the hot metal object met the coolness of the water.

"Hello, Walter," the man greeted my father as he wiped his sweaty, grime encrusted hands on a rag. "I assume this must be the young lad we were talking about a short while ago?"

"Aye, that he is, and we're ready to go ahead with the sword for him that we talked about."

"Well good. I'm just finishing up a job and I can start on his sword today. He can pick it up next Wednesday if you want."

"That would be grand," my father replied. "Is that agreeable with you, Campbell?"

"That's braw!" I enthusiastically replied. Then turning to the swordsmith asked, "If it's not too much trouble, Mr. Wilkinson, would it be ok if I came back here when you start on my sword so I can see it from the very beginning?"

"That's fine Campbell," George answered with a smile on his face. "I'll start on your sword right after my noonday meal. If you can be back here then you're more than welcome to watch."

"Thank you, Mr. Wilkinson. If my father has no objections, I'll be back here then."

My father had no objections. He said I could stay as long as I wanted and he would see me back at Inverquharity. So shortly after noon I was back in the swordsmith's shop. I had only intended to stay a short while but ended up staying most of the afternoon.

Watching the swordsmith was watching a true artist at work. He started with various pieces of iron and steel rods that he heated to just the right color. Then with his hammer and tongs he would twist, bend and fold the rods together into a workable mass that he pounded with his hammer. Moving the block of glowing metal back and forth between his coal furnace and the anvil, George repeatedly hammered and reheated the mass of iron and steel until it began to take the shape of something manmade.

After getting the metal the length, thickness and width he wanted George then began working the sides, edges and handle into the shape of a sword. I was in awe watching something forged from fire and metal into an object that was both beautiful as well as lethal.

It was late in the day when George set aside his tools. He then began cleaning his sweaty grime and soot encrusted hands with a rag as he said, "Well, lad, it's time for me to have my evening meal. If you come back late Wednesday morning I should have your sword finished."

"Thank you, Mr. Wilkinson," I replied. "I'll be back before noon on Wednesday."

"I'll have it ready for you, and Campbell," George continued with a smile on his face, "now that you're old enough to carry a nice weapon like this you're old enough to address me by my given name."

"Thank you, George," I hesitantly replied as I turned and left the shop.

I hadn't taken many steps when I heard a loud hateful voice that I instantly recognized and it made my blood run cold. I quickly ducked into the space between the swordsmith's shop and an adjacent building. Coming out of a tavern just down the street, staggering would be a better description, was none other than Alexander Lindsay with two other men. It was fortunate Lindsay was talking loudly so that I heard his voice in time to react because I wouldn't have recognized him. The sparse beard he was wearing the last time I had seen him had now grown into a full, bushy beard that completely concealed the scar I had given him as well as the rest of his face. The only part of Lindsay's face that I recognized from before were his eyes. The beard had changed his facial appearance completely, except for those dark eyes with their menacing glare.

One of the others I recognized as the man Sande had swatted with the side of his sword, the other I had never seen before. Fortunately for me, they were all so besotted with drink that they didn't recognize or even see me. I stayed hidden until they had walked out of sight. Breathing a silent prayer of thanks for my narrow escape, I quickly mounted my horse and rode back to Inverquharity.

Chapter 5

Early the next morning, which was Tuesday, I set out for Balmanoch to join the others. When I left Inverquharity, the sun was shining brightly, producing a good deal of warmth. About halfway to my destination, however, the weather changed. The sun disappeared behind some clouds and a light rain started to fall. I wrapped my cloak tightly about me to protect against the now chilly temperatures and drizzle. The wet was just beginning to soak through my cloak when I arrived at my destination. I was glad to see smoke coming from the chimney in the barn since that offered the promise of some relief from the cold and wet.

In spite of the cold drizzle, there was a lot of activity at Balmanoch. There was a grassy area in front of the barn that had a large number of men practicing movements with assorted weaponry. Others were carrying tools and lumber in and out of the barn.

After wrapping Malice's reins around a post, I walked into the barn and was gratified to see a roaring fire in the fireplace. After my long and chilly ride the warmth emanating from the fireplace was most welcome. Duncan, Malcome and James were there. The three of them along with several others were busily occupied in assembling benches and cots. No one noticed me when I first came in so I took some time to warm up in front of the fireplace. After a few minutes, I walked over to where all the activity was taking place.

"Hello, lads," I greeted everyone.

"Ah, Campbeel, sae guid ay ye tae make an appearance. An' yoo've timed it jist reit, jist abit aw th' wark involved in gettin' sit up haur has bin dain," Duncan said to me sarcastically but with a friendly smile on his face.

After some more good-natured ribbing about how I had ducked out on my share of the work of moving, Duncan showed me around our new facility. The barn was constructed with thick sandstone walls and the wooden rafters were covered with good quality slate. Even though the structure was old it was well made and weather tight. It was also quite large. There was room enough for 30 cots at one end and enough space for tables and benches at the end near the fireplace that could seat up to 50 people.

The end of the barn near where the cots were set up was made of wood. At one time there had been a large doorway there for the animals in the barn but it had long since fallen into disrepair and been boarded up. The entrance that was used now was a smaller one not far from the fireplace.

There was a second building about 50 feet from the barn. It was constructed in a similar fashion with the same materials as the barn although it was much smaller. This was used as a stable for those in our camp that had horses.

These were the only two usable structures on the farm although the ruins of what had once been a tower castle were in evidence as well as the ruins of smaller structures that had probably been dwellings or storage cribs. The location of less than two miles from Arbroath along with the ample land area and two usable buildings made Balmanoch ideal for our purposes.

At noon, when the training was over for the day, Sande and Philip joined the four of us for a midday meal. We sat at one of the tables in front of the fireplace, shaking off the chill of the mornings drizzle as we enjoyed freshly killed venison and oat cakes.

It was during our meal that I told everyone about the new sword I was picking up in the morning and about my near encounter with Lindsay the previous day. I was at first hesitant about telling everyone about my new sword since I was concerned it might cause some jealously. It turned out I didn't need to worry about that. Everyone seemed genuinely happy for me. In fact, the only concern anyone of our group expressed was about my near encounter with Lindsay.

"I want you to take a couple of men with you to get your sword," Sande told me.

"I'll be fine. I don't need anyone with me," I answered with a confidence I really didn't feel.

"I'm sure you'll be fine but I still want a couple of our lads to go with you," Sande insisted.

I could have refused the company and gone alone if I wanted, but in truth I was concerned about running into Lindsay again. Malcome and Duncan offered to go with me and I accepted their offer without too many more protestations.

The next morning the three of us set out for Forfar. We arrived at the swordsmith's shop in the late morning. As soon as we entered the shop, George saw us and put down his hammer and tongs and greeted us with a friendly smile. Reaching out to a shelf behind his anvil, he brought out an object wrapped in an old blanket. Laying the object on a counter the three of us watched as he began to carefully unwrap it. When he at last had completely unwrapped the object in the blanket, he stepped back saying, "Well, Campbell, what do you think?"

For several seconds I was too dazzled by the sword lying on the counter in front of me to speak. It was hard to believe that something that was designed to kill someone could be so incredibly beautiful. The blade, which was polished to a bright shine, had beautiful intricate patterns that ran along its entire length. The tang was covered with a dark oak handle that also had been polished to a bright finish. The hand guard was a V-shaped piece of hardened steel with two balls on the end. The sturdy stems of the hand guard were stout enough to stop any enemy sword swings and the two balls on the ends could be used as an offensive weapon in close combat. It was truly the work of a very accomplished swordsmith.

Finally coming to my senses, I gingerly reached out to touch my sword. I rubbed my fingers along the blade down to the handle and picked it up. It was constructed like a standard claymore but it was actually a bit shorter and lighter. It was still heavy enough and long enough to swing and slash with two hands, as most claymores were used, but it was also light enough to use with one hand either thrusting or swinging. Being able to use a sword with one hand gave me the added benefit of being able to hold a shield or different weapon in my free hand.

As I raised the sword above my head, the blade caught a ray of sunlight that was coming through a crack in the wall. The sunlight was reflected all around the shop as I rotated the sword in my hand. The sunlight reflecting off the blade gave the sword an almost mystical quality. Finding my voice I finally answered George by saying, "Yes, I think this is very nice indeed," as I continued to admire the sword.

Leaving us for a minute, George came back with a leather belt and scabbard for my sword. The odor of freshly tanned and cured leather wafted into my nostrils as I fastened the belt tightly about my waist and placed the sword in the scabbard.

"Thank you, George," I told the swordsmith as I handed him a bag of silver coins my father had given me to pay for the sword.

'Thank you, Campbell, and please thank your father for me. Wear your sword proudly and may it serve you well in the years to come."

We said our goodbyes to George and the three of us set out on the trip back to Balmanoch. It was an uneventful journey. There was no sign of Lindsay or his cronies in town or on the way back. To be honest, I was a bit sorry I didn't see him. With my new sword at my side along with the training I had received from Sande, I felt confident in my abilities to handle myself well in a conflict. In addition, I knew Malcome and Duncan were loyal and tough friends who would acquit themselves well in a fight. It wasn't that I wanted to kill someone, but rather that I wanted to prove my worth in combat and, if I did have to kill someone, it might as well be Lindsay.

The training went well at Balmanoch and I soon found myself spending as much time there as I did at Inverquharity. Sande was in charge of our training and Philip took Sande's place whenever Sande was called away. The four of us, Duncan, Malcome, James and I were Sande and Philip's assistants. We took turns training the newer people on different weapons under the watchful gaze of Sande and Philip.

It wasn't too many months later that I would get my chance to prove myself in combat. On that day I felt the fear, anger, and exhilaration of being in battle. That was the day I killed my first man in mortal conflict and ironically I didn't use my new sword to kill him.

Chapter 6

It was on the morning of the sixteenth day of January that word came to us while we were training that a group of well-armed men had landed on the beach just north of Arbroath. A man on horseback came galloping into our camp on a lathered, panting horse, and he excitedly told us these men were attacking the town and asked Sande if our group could render aid.

"How many men are there and do you know who they are or where they're from?" Sande asked.

"About 20, maybe more. They look like they're from the North. They arrived in a boat that they beached just north of town. They could be Vikings. At least they have long blond hair and are dressed as Vikings looked in a painting I saw once," the rider replied. "We need help and we need it quickly. They've already killed at least one merchant who tried to resist them and they're threatening to burn the town down."

"We'll be glad to help," Sande answered. He then turned to us saying, "Lads, now is the time to show everyone how well you've learned your lessons here. Grab your weapons and form up on the practice field."

Turning to Philip he said, "Divide the men into two equal groups. I'll take one group and approach the town from along the coast to prevent these Vikings, or whoever they are, from escaping. We'll first burn their boat then proceed into town to attack them. You take your group in a northerly direction till you hit Aberbrothock Burn then follow the burn in an easterly direction till you come to Saint Vigeans church. Once you get to the church get to some high ground and wait until you see the smoke from the ship that we're going to set on fire. Once you see the smoke come charging into town as fast as you can. I don't imagine the intruders are even aware we're in the vicinity so we should take them by surprise from two directions."

"Sande," Philip spoke, "how dae yi'll waant us tae proceed wance we catch up wi' th' pirates? Shuid we tak' prisoners or shuid we save th' crown th' expense o' a trial?"

"Take prisoners if the pirates offer no resistance and surrender peaceably, but if they resist kill them on the spot," Sande responded forcefully. "Good luck to all of you and remember your training."

Duncan and I were assigned to the group with Philip. Malcome and James went with Sande. Since our camp was only a short distance from the beach Sande and his group set out on foot. The rest of us mounted our horses and went at a fast pace until we reached St. Vigeans. We rode around the church at a full gallop, our horses' hooves throwing up sand and gravel. We then rode up the hill that lies just to the south, and there we paused to wait for the smoke from the burning ship.

There was already smoke in the air when we reached the top of the hill, and orange flickers of fire as well, but we quickly saw that was from buildings in Arbroath that the invaders had put to the torch. We stayed there for what seemed an eternity, although it was probably only a few minutes, before we saw the first wisps of smoke rising from the beach.

Upon seeing the smoke from the beach Philip drew his sword, faced us and screamed, "Noo lads! Dae yer duty n' pat th' pirates tae th' sword!" His horse, catching the excitement from his rider, reared back on its hind legs then charged forward, the rest of us following behind.

I was riding next to Duncan and was glad to have him in close proximity. Not only was he the best man with a spear but was the biggest man in our group. In addition to his spear, Duncan carried a sword but he kept that in his scabbard. With one hand on the reins of his horse, he held the spear out in front of him with the other.

I was carrying my sword and had also tucked my axe into the leather belt that held my scabbard. Following the lead of Philip, I had my new sword drawn, ready to strike down any enemy that came within my range.

My breath was coming quickly now, quick deep breaths that were more from excitement than from exertion. I remember being afraid, but I think I was more afraid of failing to do well in the coming fight than I was of any injury to myself. I was too young to know the danger I was heading into. To me, it was a stoatin adventure.

We quickly reached the Carnie Loan road and headed straight towards the smoke and flames of the burning buildings. As we passed a large cathedral on our left, Arbroath Abbey, we saw that the burning buildings were located in the area that the locals called the "fit o' the toon," which was the harbor area.

There were at least four buildings on fire. Two were fishermen's huts on the north side of the harbor. These were wooden structures and they were both fully engulfed in flames. The other two buildings that were on fire were on Ladybridge Street, which ran in front of the harbor a short distance from the fishermen's huts. These were stone buildings and were not as fully engulfed as the fisherman's huts.

As we got closer the smoke began to envelop us and the visibility became very poor. A short way ahead of us, I saw a figure leave a building carrying a sack that appeared quite heavy, a crossbow was slung across his back and a sword hung at his waist. Judging from the long blondish hair and manner of dress, I knew this person had to be one of the people we were after. His back was to us and he was not aware of our presence, the crackling and burning of the fires drowning out any sounds our horses hooves were making.

As Philip reached the man he shouted, "Raise yer hauns n' surrender or die!" The man dropped the sack he was carrying but he showed no sign of surrender. He whirled around, drawing his sword as he did so and drew back in order to strike a blow at Alansoun. However Philip was much quicker than his adversary. He swung his sword with such accurate ferocity, that coupled with the velocity he was traveling, caused the blade of his sword to completely sever the man's head in a single swipe.

The head hit the ground and rolled for some distance before stopping, its eyes still open and the mouth opening and closing as if in protest at the violence it had just suffered. The lifeless body stood erect for a few seconds, with blood gushing from the neck, before it dropped to its knees. It then fell backwards, the sword still grasped firmly in the lifeless hand. It was then I noticed a most curious happening. The long blond hair separated from the head and lay by itself. The man had been wearing a wig.

Before I had time to think any more about this development we became fully surrounded by the smoke and the visibility was so bad that the horses were of no use to us. Philip ordered us to dismount which we quickly did and formed up around him. "Follow me noo lads bit bade claise," Philip began, "there's na telling how many mair o' thae rascals we'll…" He suddenly stopped talking as the head of a crossbow bolt appeared from the center of his chest and blood began spreading all over the front of his tunic. With a look of surprise he slumped to the ground.

Two more bolts came whizzing through the air, one passed

harmlessly overhead while the other struck a man standing next to me in the upper leg. We looked in the direction from where the bolts had come and we saw a group of 9 or 10 men, three had cross bows in their hands and the rest were armed with swords. Most of them had long blond hair and were dressed in the same style as in descriptions I'd heard of how Viking warriors looked.

It was at that moment that all the fear I had vanished. It was replaced with an uncontrollable rage. I drew my sword as did others in our group and we charged forward toward the group yelling and screaming as we went.

The crossbow men were frantically trying to reload their weapons but only one was able to get off a shot before our group was upon them. That shot struck the cobblestone street and glanced harmlessly away. Then our swords were slashing downward. The sound of swords and shields smashing against each other filled the street with a deafening sound.

I was slashing at one of the enemy with my sword but my swings were being blocked by my adversary's shield. Through the smoke I could see that this person was wearing a blonde haired wig, the same as the man that Philip had dispatched a short while ago. He suddenly lunged forward, knocking me off my feet and I landed flat on my back, losing my sword in the process. Looking up, I saw my foe raise his sword, preparing to deliver a killing blow, his face contorted in a mixture of hate and anger.

It was then that I recognized the man standing over me as one of the people that had attacked me in Dundee that day when Sande had come to my rescue. In that same instant, a look of recognition crossed his face as well. "I know you," I blurted out and my outburst seemed to cause my assailant to check his swing.

"And I know you as well. It's a pity you won't live to tell anyone you saw me," he replied as his sword began arcing down towards me.

A split second before the sword struck my chest a spear came flashing through the smoke striking the sword and causing the swing to go wide, hitting the ground next to me. Saying a quick prayer of thanks for Duncan's skill with a spear, I quickly grabbed my axe from my waistband. Before my adversary had a chance to recover I swung the axe with all my might at his ankle. I can still remember the immense sense of satisfaction I had when I felt the axe cut deeply into his leg, breaking his ankle and causing my foe to drop to his knees.

Screaming in pain and outrage he produced a knife from his side and tried to stab me with it. However I was already swinging my axe and the flat side of it hit him fully on the right side of his face before the knife could find its mark. Blood, teeth and spittle flew out of his mouth, and he sat where he was, looking dumbfounded and amazed, blood gushing from the gaping wound where his mouth used to be. Using both hands in a quick backhand motion I quickly swung my axe again, this time striking the left side of his forehead with the blade portion of the axe. It seemed as though his entire head exploded and I was drenched in a shower of blood and brains. My assailant fell backwards, his dead body twitching and contorting in its death throes.

I quickly grabbed my sword and scrambled to my feet. By that time Sande and the rest of the group had joined us. We put our training to good use; slicing, hacking, cutting, parrying and thrusting with all the weapons at our disposal as we had been taught.

Together our combined force proved more than a match for the intruders. Our foes had had enough and were backing away into the smoke. As they were leaving a slight breeze caused the smoke to clear a bit and I caught a glance of another familiar face. This face sported a full bushy beard. It was the face of Alexander Lindsay.

Chapter 7

I was wearing a good portion of the brains and blood of the man I had slain. I was trying to clean myself up the best I could when Duncan ran up to me. "Urr ye a' richt Campbell? Fur a while thare ah thought ye wur a gonner," he said in a concerned voice.

"I'm fine, thanks to you. That was an amazing throw, hitting that man's sword with your spear as you did. "

"Ah, weel actually ah wis aiming at his heid. Tis lik' everything else though, if ye cannae be guid then be jammy," William replied with a grin.

"How are you lads doing?" I heard a voice behind me say and turned to see Sande walking toward us. "Ah, Campbell, I hope that blood and guts you're wearing didn't come from you," he continued.

"I'm fine, thanks to Duncan's skill with a spear," I answered.

"We're all mostly braw, except fur puir Philip. Ah think we gave a lot mair than we teuk though," Duncan interjected.

In addition to the men slain by Philip and myself, there was a third man lying prostate. Two separate blood trails following the path that our adversaries had taken gave evidence that two more of their group had suffered injuries. In addition to losing Philip, we had three men with injuries, none life threatening.

Looking at the blood trails, Sande said, "You lads have acquitted yourselves well but there's still work to be done. Let's follow those blood trails and round up the rest of that group." Sande detailed two of our group to stay behind and assist the wounded. The rest of us set off with him following the blood trails.

Catching up with Sande, I said, "May I have a word with you?"

"What is it, Campbell?"

"Well Sande, those weren't Vikings. They were men from close by dressed to look like Vikings. In fact the man that I killed was one of them that attacked me in Dundee. I also got a look at who I think was their leader; it was Alexander Lindsay."

Sande turned and looked at me sharply, "That's a very serious accusation to make, Campbell. As you know the Lindsays are a very powerful family and Alexander's father is the Justiciar. The Lindsays won't take kindly to anyone that accuses one of them of a crime such as this."

"I wouldn't make a charge such as this unless I was positive," I replied.

"There was a lot of smoke back there. You may have seen someone that just looks like Lindsay and, as far as the man you killed, well, his own mother wouldn't recognize him now with the mess you made of his face. A bit of advice, Campbell, let's keep this to ourselves for the time being. Hopefully, we'll apprehend the rest of this gang but until we do let's not accuse anyone without more proof."

"Aye," I replied. I was disappointed with Sande's answer but I knew he was right. We would need more than my testimony to make a case against Alexander Lindsay.

We continued following the blood trail and it led us into town and stopped at the west gate entrance of the abbey. We pounded on the door without any answer. We yelled loudly and pounded some more until we heard the sound of a bar being lifted and the door slowly swung open.

A young monk with an apprehensive look on his face stood in the doorway and inquired as to what we wanted. We explained what had happened and asked for permission to enter the abbey to search for the rest of the gang. The priest nervously looked at us both and said, "This abbey is sacred ground, I must ask the abbot. Please wait here."

The door was closed again and we could hear the bar being put back in place. Several minutes later the door was opened again. This time the monk was joined by none other than Alexander Lindsay himself.

"What are you doing here and why are you disturbing us?" Lindsay asked.

"We're looking for a band of thieves and murderers that attacked Arbroath. They've robbed and killed. I'm sure you've seen the smoke from the fires they've set. Their trail leads here, to this very door. They must be inside. Stand aside and let us come in and search for them," Sande replied.

"I can assure you they are not here," Lindsay said, not at all convincingly, "and even if they are here this is a church and they have sanctuary."

"Sanctuary or not we have reason to believe they're here. Now stand aside, were coming in." With that Sande pushed Lindsay aside and led our group inside the gate.

Lindsay did not try and stop us; instead he turned and walked away toward the abbot's quarters.

"Spread out and search the grounds," Sande told us and we promptly began to search the grounds of the abbey.

While we were searching, Lindsay returned along with Abbot Walter. They went up to Sande and the abbot said, "My name is Abbot Walter. Welcome to God's house. It appears that you are in charge of these men. Who do I have the pleasure of addressing?"

"My name is Alexander Seton. By the authority and permission of our King James, through his regent Sir Alexander Livingston of Callander, I have been in charge of training local men for possible service in our king's common army. My men and I are in pursuit of a group of men, dressed as Vikings that have robbed and burned part of the town. We have reason to believe they may be in the abbey."

"Order them off the premises, Abbot," Lindsay interjected. "They have no right to be here. I told them as much but they barged in anyway."

"I'll decide who has a right to be here and who doesn't," the abbot replied. Turning to Sande, he said, "I hope you apprehend these people. You are welcome to search anywhere in the abbey, however if those ruffians were here they are probably gone by now. There are lots of entrances and exits from here that most people don't know about." Upon saying this last bit, the abbot turned his head and glared at Lindsay.

"I protest!" Lindsay loudly proclaimed, ignoring the look Abbot Walter had given him. "The Justiciar of Angus has the right to use the open areas of the abbey and has the right to allow or forbid who he chooses to be here."

"And when you become Justiciar, then you can exercise that right," the abbot coolly responded. "Until that time, as a favor to your father, you are welcome to stay here but I'll decide who else is welcome and who is not."

Turning to Sande, the abbot bowed and said, "It was a pleasure to meet you, sir. You and your men are welcome here anytime. If I can assist you in anyway please let me know."

"Thank you, Abbot," Sande said, returning the bow. "My men will be through with our search and be out of your way as soon as possible."

"Take your time," Abbot Walter responded as he turned and walked away.

Lindsay started to follow him when he noticed me for the first time. With a hate filled voice he said, "Well, well, little Ogilvy, Judging from your blood spattered clothing it looks as though you were in the thick of it. It's amazing how brave you are when your protector is close by."

"And it's amazing how well that beard covers up that scar on your ugly face," I retorted.

Lindsay's face darkened. For a second I thought he was going to draw his sword, but he controlled his anger and said, "Perhaps I'll have the pleasure of meeting you again sometime soon, preferably when you aren't with your companions." Then he stalked away.

Sande and I watched as Lindsay walked away. Then Sande turned to me and said, "I think you're right, Campbell. If Lindsay wasn't the leader of that group then he was certainly involved with them. I think we've made a dangerous enemy in Lindsay."

I nodded in agreement just as the rest of our group was coming back. James was in the lead and he was carrying something in his hand. "They aren't here now Sande, but I'm sure they were here. We found more blood and also this," James said as he held up a blond haired wig that was covered in blood.

"Well now we know for sure they were here," Sande said.

"Shouldn't we contact th' authorities?" Duncan asked, as he joined us.

"Would do no good, the authority in this county is David Lindsay and it would not be worthwhile reporting to him since it appears his son is deeply involved," Sande explained. "I think we've done all we can here, lads," Sande went on. "Let's get our wounded taken care of and see if we can render any aid to any of the townsfolk that were harmed by these outlaws."

The three men in our group had been patched up somewhat by the time we got back. The men that Sande had left with our wounded had managed to get the arrow out of the man's leg that had been shot and a bandage wrapped around the wounds. The other two, one with a slashing wound to the chest and the other a stab wound to the upper leg, had makeshift bandages around their wounds. The wounds were still bleeding and open and they needed further medical attention.

"We need to get these men to a doctor. Does anyone know a doctor that's close by?" Sande asked.

"Nae doctur aroond 'at ah ken," Malcome replied. "But Ah ken th' nam ay a healer that's better than onie doctur. 'Er nam is Morag Macpherson. She's a bit odd but there's nae finer healer around."

"Ah, not Morag," James said, "she's a witch."

"Witch ur nae she can heal th' hurts ay mannie ur beest," Malcome persisted.

"Why do you say she's a witch?" I asked James.

"She can do strange things," James explained. "She can make you hear birds singing when there's nary a bird around and she conjures up savages from thin air. Late at night people say you can hear drums and loud chanting coming from her house. So loud it could only be made by a whole tribe of savages."

"The only thing I'm concerned with is if she can help our

wounded," Sande said. "Campbell, you, James, Duncan and Malcome take the wounded to this Morag. The rest of you take the dead somewhere they can get a proper burial and then help anyone that needs it."

The four of us promptly commandeered a wagon and set off with the wounded to see Morag Macpherson.

Chapter 8

Morag lived just off the road that leads from Arbroath to Brechin, about four miles from Arbroath.

Duncan and I rode our horses and James drove the wagon with Malcome in the back with our wounded. Since the road was not at all smooth, we went slowly to make the ride as painless as possible for our passengers.

We still made good time and were within sight of Morag's house in just over an hour. Her house was actually visible from a long distance away since it was quite large.

As we turned off the road to go up to the house, I remember being impressed with both the size and construction of the dwelling. It looked more like a castle than a house. It was a two story square building made out of grey stone with turrets on the northwest and southeast corners. The grey stone was unusual since most stone structures in that area were made out of the reddish sandstone that was quarried locally. The shape of the house along with the grey stone gave the structure a mysterious almost foreboding look.

We halted our wagon near the front entrance. I went to the massive front door to knock but before my hand had touched the door, it suddenly opened with a loud creak. A short wrinkled woman with long, white hair that hung down to her waist was standing in the doorway.

"Ma'am, my name is Campbell Ogilvy and we've come—"

"Yes, yes, I know why you're here," Morag said, cutting me off with a laugh that sounded more like a cackle. "Don't just stand there, come in, come in, and bring your wounded with you."

We quickly did as instructed and we stepped over the threshold into what was a small dark room with an unlit fireplace against the far wall. A single candle was burning on a table against a wall which helped to add some light to the room. The only other light in the room came from a small window just to the right of the door.

"This way, this way," Morag said, as she motioned us to follow her through an archway on the other side of the room that led into a long hallway. The hallway was windowless and was lit by a single candle that didn't help much to alleviate the gloom. We followed her down the dimly lit corridor, our feet producing an eerie echo against the stone walls, until she stopped in front of an oaken door that was secured with a large lock. Producing a key from her pocket, she undid the lock and pushed the door open. "In here," she instructed us as she walked through the doorway.

We followed Morag into what was probably the most unusual room I've ever seen. It was a large room with several windows that enabled the room to be well lit. What made the room unusual were the furnishings. The first thing I saw was a human skeleton standing upright against the far wall. A shelf that ran along the far wall was filled with glass jars that contained a lot of unusual items, some of which appeared to be human organs. One large jar contained the entire head of some unfortunate chap that appeared to have suffered from some sort of serious disease that caused his entire nose and right cheek to have been eaten away.

There were rafters in the ceiling that had numerous items hanging from them. In addition to many different varieties of herbs and other plants, there appeared to be numerous small animals, bats and reptiles that were dried and preserved. I was somewhat taken aback to see that there were also what appeared to be human heads hanging from the rafters that had been somehow shrunk to the size of a man's fist.

To the left of the doorway we had come through was a large rectangular platform under a window. The platform was covered with straw underneath a large piece of white linen. Morag motioned for us to help our wounded comrades onto this platform. Once they were on the platform we made them as comfortable as possible and Morag began to treat them.

She went first to Willie, the man with the long gash across his chest. After a quick exam, she suddenly turned and called out loudly, "Surena, bring me a needle and horse hair and also a sponge and cleaning ointment." She went back to examining the gash. In a very short while one of the most beautiful women I've ever seen entered the room. She was carrying a tray with the items on it that Morag had called for.

We all watched as this beauty walked into the room to set the tray on a small table near the platform. She appeared to be about 20 years old and was tall and thin with a dark complexion. Her hair was jet black and hung down to her waist. Her eyes were the same color as her skin and seemed to sparkle. She smiled as she entered the room, her voluptuous lips parting to reveal bright perfectly formed teeth.

"Ah," Morag exclaimed with another of her laughs that sounded like a cackle as she noticed that we were all staring at the woman. "I see you also appreciate my daughter's beauty."

"Aye, we do. She is a lovely lass," agreed James. "Please forgive us for staring."

"Quite all right," replied Morag as she began to clean Willie's wound with the sponge she had moistened with the ointment. "This might sting a mite," she told Willie before she began rubbing the sponge across the gash. The scream of pain that Willie made when the sponge touched the gash proved her right.

"Surena is not from around here as you can probably tell," Morag went on to explain. "I was in Persia a few years ago and brought her back from there. She's not my actual daughter, although I've come to love her as if she was."

"Hoo did ye manage tae travel aw th' way frae haur tae Pursia?" Malcome asked.

"A few years ago," Morag began, "a sea captain wanted a doctor to travel with him in order to take care of his crew for the long voyage to and from the Far East. The captain's previous voyage was a disaster. Over half his crew died of the plague and he wanted to do everything he could to prevent something like that from happening again. However, no doctor was willing to go on such a long and dangerous voyage. When I heard of the problem, I went to see this captain. I told him that I was willing to go and that I was the best healer around, as good as or better than any doctor.

"The Captain was a very fine gentlemen but wasn't in favor of taking a woman with him. Seafarers are a superstitious lot and the Captain was no exception. They think it bad luck to have a woman onboard a ship. However when I told the Captain that in addition to being able to heal the sick I knew of some spells and chants that would ensure a safe trip for him and his crew that changed his mind. I ended up sailing with him to the Far East and while I was there I was able to buy Surena for the equivalent of 25 camels."

Noticing our surprised look Morag went on to explain, "Buying and selling people in that part of the world is quite normal and acceptable. In the case of Surena she was a rebellious slave girl who was owned by a sultan that couldn't control her. The more he beat her, the more she rebelled."

By this time, Morag had cleaned the wound and now produced a large needle that was threaded with the horse hair. "Best hold him down while I sew this wound closed," she said as she bent over Willie whose eyes were now opened wide with fear.

Duncan grabbed both of Willie's feet and James and I each grabbed an arm as Morag began to insert the needle into the torn parts of Willie's flesh.

"Nae! Nae! I don't need to be sewn up," Willie protested as he felt the needle going through his skin. His protests quickly turned to agonized cries of pain and shouted curses and it took all our strength to hold him down.

Fortunately for us all, Morag was good at her work and the stitching was done quickly. She then applied a salve over her handiwork and covered it with a linen bandage. "Good as new," she exclaimed when she was done. "Change the bandage every couple of days and apply this salve every day and your friend will be right as rain in 10 days. The stiches should fall out on their own but if not you can take them out yourself."

"If ye dornt min' mah askin', hoo did ye get twenty and five camels?" Duncan asked as soon as Willie had quieted down.

"Don't mind ye asking atall," Morag said with another of her cackling laughs. "While we were in port taking on goods to bring back here, we heard that this Sultan's favorite wife was seriously ill with severe stomach pains. The pain had gone on for weeks and this sultan was so worried about his favorite wife that he was offering 100 camels to anyone that could cure her."

"I had the Captain send word to the Sultan that I might be able to help and I was soon in the palace examining this women. Turns out all that was ailing her was she was constipated. Completely blocked up she was. I gave her my special potion of citrate mixed with magnesium. That cleaned her out proper and she was right as rain in less than 12 hours."

Morag gave out another of her cackles before continuing, "While I was in the palace I saw Surena and heard that the Sultan was ready to behead her for her disobedience. I realized that this was an opportunity for Surena and also for me. I wanted someone to assist me and to pass my healing secrets on to and Surena was definitely someone who needed rescuing. So after the Sultan saw that his wife was cured and we got our 100 camels I had the Captain ask the Sultan if he would sell Surena. The captain had to handle all the business since the Sultan wouldn't even talk to a woman. We haggled a bit but in the end the Sultan took 25 camels back in exchange for Surena. The other 75 camels we were able to sell for gold. I split the gold with the Captain. With my share I returned here with Surena and built this nice house."

"Well I'd say Surena was certainly a good buy," I agreed.

"That she was," Morag said with another cackle as she moved to treat our other friends. She cleaned their wounds and packed them with cobwebs that she took out of a large container. She then smeared the same salve over the wounds as she had put on Willie. "The cobwebs keep the pus away," She exclaimed before wrapping bandages around both their wounds. "Make sure you put the salve on daily and change the bandages every two days," she instructed. "They'll be good as new in 10 days as well".

"Thank you Ma'am, I'll make sure your instructions are followed," I said as I handed her the silver coins that Sande had given me to pay her with. "One more thing before we go. How did you know we were coming?"

"I have a friend named Gavan who is a butcher in Arbroath. He stopped here on his way to Brechin with a wagonload of beef. He told me that Arbroath had been attacked by Vikings or pirates but that you lads had repulsed them. He said that you were bringing a wagonload of your wounded to me to be treated."

"Well there was an attack but it wasn't pirates or Vikings, it was the Justiciar's son, Alexander Lindsay, and his band of cutthroats. They were trying to make people think it was pirates or Vikings."

"I should have known," Morag said. "Alexander Lindsay is a very bad man indeed. His father is as fine a man as you'll find anywhere but his son is the complete opposite. I guess you've heard he murdered a man in Paris, that's why he had to leave the school he was enrolled in there?"

"I hadn't heard that but it doesn't surprise me," I replied. "Well thank you for all you've done, it's very much appreciated."

"You're more than welcome," Morag said. "Have a safe trip back to Arbroath and be very careful of young Lindsay; he's a dangerous enemy to have."

"I'll be careful. Thank you again," I said before getting on my horse for the trip back to Arbroath.

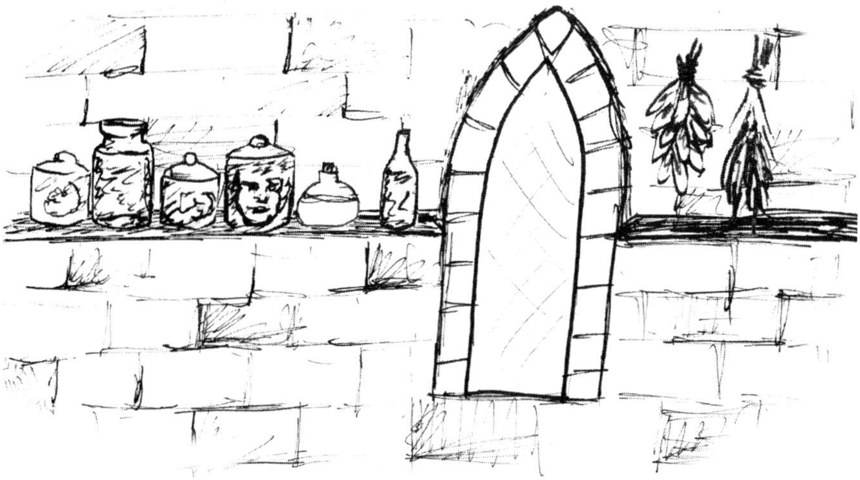

Chapter 9

The trip back to Arbroath was uneventful. We arrived an hour or two after dark. To our surprise, we arrived in the middle of a full celebration. It was even more of a surprise to find out that those of us that had fought off the raiders were the center of the festivities. It seemed as if the entire population of Arbroath as well as the county of Angus itself had turned out to celebrate their deliverance from the intruders.

Bonfires were blazing every few yards in the middle of the High Street, the burning wood sending sparks upward into the night sky. Flaming torches illuminated the street from the abbey all the way to the seawall.

Carcasses of deer, cow and sheep were cooking on spits over the bonfires and there were ample supplies of wine and ale. Everyone that had helped in the rescue of the town was there and most of them appeared to have already sampled their share of the spirits.

As soon as our wagon was spied coming into town a large contingent of the revelers came out to meet us and we were given a hero's welcome. Mugs of ale were thrust into our hands and plates of the cooked delicacies, hot and steaming from the fire, were offered to us.

Our wounded were helped down from the wagon and given seats near one of the bonfires. They were waited on by the townsfolk who kept them well supplied with food and drink.

The four of us made our way through the crowd, receiving many congratulations and pats on the back from the celebrants. Duncan and I had large mugs of ale and Malcome and James had a flagon of wine each and all four of us had plates piled high with food. We found seats on some steps and quickly devoured our repast.

James finished his food first and I saw him strike up a conversation with a pretty lass that had been bringing out plates of food to set on the tables. It wasn't long before the two of them walked off together.

The rest of us were just planning to go back for refills when I saw Sande heading our way along with my father. They were in the company of a well-dressed middle aged man and a young woman that I judged to be his daughter. The man was dressed in a kilt and linen shirt and wore a blue cloak trimmed in red velvet that hung almost to the ground. The woman was also well dressed. She wore a full length red dress that fitted her perfectly underneath a black cloak that was trimmed in red fox fur.

"Hello lads," Sande greeted us. "I'm glad to see you all made it back safely. As you can see the townsfolk are most appreciative of what we did." Motioning to my father, who was standing behind him with a large grin on his face, Sande continued, "Campbell, I told your dad how well you acquitted yourself today."

"I'm very proud of you, Campbell," my dad interjected. "Sande told me you did your share of the fighting today. I'm proud of you and even more thankful that you came through all that without a scratch."

I managed to mumble a few words of thanks, acutely aware that my face must be bright red from the compliments.

"Let me introduce my friend," my father went on. "This is Laird George Fowler. George has an estate near Perth; Balanthrot is the name of it. He and his daughter arrived for a visit yesterday. When we heard the news about the difficulties here, and how you lads had come to the rescue, we came right up."

I shook hands with Laird Fowler who pumped my hand vigorously as he said, "It is indeed an honor to make the acquaintance of a real hero. I understand you personally were able to dispatch one of the rogues today." Before I had a chance to reply, the Laird had turned and took his daughter by the arm and guided her forward. "This is my eldest daughter, Ellene," he continued as a way of introduction.

Ellene smiled, shyly extended her hand while making a slight bow, "A pleasure to meet you, Campbell," she said in a very soft voice.

"The pleasure is entirely mine," I stammered in reply as I took her hand. Ellene raised her head, looked directly into my eyes and smiled. I don't know if it was the ale or Ellene's beauty or a combination of the two but the moment her eyes met mine, I fell totally and completely in love.

And Ellene was a beauty. She was tall and thin with a graceful way of walking that reminded me of a deer moving in the forest. Her eyes were a vibrant shade of blue in a lovely face framed by long blonde hair that hung in plaits on either side of her body.

"How long will you and your father be in the area?" I asked.

"For about a week," she replied. "My father has business in this area and your family has been nice enough to invite us to stay with them while we're here."

"We should be moving along," Sande said. "Your father and I have to see Abbot Walter at the abbey before it gets too late."

"We won't be long, Campbell," my father said. "I'll be back after we've seen the abbot."

I said my goodbyes and was rewarded with another smile from Ellene who said, "Maybe we'll meet again before we return home to Balanthrot."

"I hope so," I replied and watched as the four of them made their way to the abbey.

"Noo that is certainly a bonnie furraw tae plow," Duncan said with a lecherous glance at Ellene.

"Ah agree, that Ellene is a field ah cuid wirk a' day," Malcome chimed in.

"I think the young lady is a proper gentlewomen and I'd appreciate it if you two kept your stupid, rude comments like that to yourself," I said with such anger in my voice it surprised me.

"Ah, ah think oor mukker Campbell haes bin smitten by the sweet Ellene," said Malcome with a smirk in his voice.

"Campbell is nae smitten. He juist wants tae be th' foremaist yin o' us tae hump her, n' thats braw by me, juist sae ah huv mah caw wi' her," Duncan said in a voice that was slurred by the ale.

It was at that moment that I did something I quickly regretted. I punched Duncan as hard as I could right in his nose. I didn't regret it because I had hurt my friend, because he deserved to be hurt. I regretted it because Duncan was a good half a foot taller and at least seven stones heavier than I was.

Other than wincing slightly from my blow Duncan didn't seem fazed in the least. Before I knew it, both of his meaty hands had grabbed my tunic and had thrown me against a wall. A slight trickle of blood was running from Duncan's nose which was now nearly touching mine as he glowered at me with fire in his eyes.

The thought of a severe beating took the anger out of me and I grabbed both of Duncan's hands in mine as I said in my most sincere voice, "Duncan, I really regret having done that. Is it to late for you to accept my apology?"

My apology seemed to take some of the anger out of Duncan's eyes. I was greatly relieved when he relaxed his grip on me a bit and said, "Ah will let ye gang this time laddie bit ye dae something lik' that again 'n' ah will rearrange yer top coupon sae yer ain mither won't recognize ye."

Satisfied that he had made his point, Duncan let me go. He then turned on his heel and walked off toward a keg of ale with Malcome close behind.

I was grateful that Malcome looked back towards me and smiled as they walked off. I felt badly that I had had a falling out with Duncan but I was proud of myself for having defended the honor of the fair Ellene. In truth I didn't feel all that bad because I knew that as soon as the ale wore off I'd probably be friends with Duncan again.

Now on my own, I walked off toward the abbey, hoping to have a chance to see Ellene again. Not too many minutes had passed when I was gratified to see the west gate door to the abbey open and my father and the others emerged.

They saw me at the same time as I saw them. My father smiled and hailed me, "Hallo Campbell, come join us."

I immediately accepted my father's invitation, but try as hard as I could; I found it impossible to take my eyes off Ellene's face or carry on a normal conversation. I was immensely happy to see that Ellene was also looking at me and we exchanged a number of shy smiles as we walked down the street.

Turning towards Sande, I summoned up the courage to ask, "Do you suppose you could do without me at Balmanoch for a few days? There are a few things at Inverquharity I'd like to take care of."

Sande smiled and glanced at Ellene who I thought blushed

slightly. "I'm sure you have lots to do, Campbell," he began, "to tell the truth, I was thinking that the way the lads conducted themselves today we can afford to take some time off from training. Besides, with the loss of Phillip we couldn't properly do all the training anyway. I need to take care of some business back home myself so feel free to go on home. We can start up again after the spring planting is over."

"Thank you, Sande," I replied. "I've enjoyed working with you; you've taught me a lot."

"It was my pleasure, Campbell; you've been an apt pupil. I'd be proud to serve with you in any army. I'm working up a list to send to King James of everyone in our group that is fit and ready to serve in his common army should the need arise. I just want you to know that your name will be at the top of that list."

"Thank you, Sande," I replied with a tremendous grin on my face. "I'll head back to Inverquharity tonight with the others. I'll go back to Balmanoch tomorrow to get the rest of my gear if that's all right."

"That will be fine," Sande replied. "However I do insist on sending a few of the fellows with your group for protection. Some of the gang that we chased off earlier might still be lurking around. We'll see you tomorrow."

"That's grand," my father said as he joined our conversation. "It will be nice to have you home again full time. Your mother and sister are always happier when you're home. Well, we should be going then; we have about a two hour ride ahead of us.

At that moment James emerged from a nearby alleyway with the young lady he had disappeared with earlier. The bits of straw sticking to their clothes indicating they had been frolicking in a nearby stable.

"James," Sande said. "If you would be so kind, please get three other men and escort Campbell and his group back to their home."

James gave his lady friend a quick kiss good-bye and went off to do as he was asked. He returned shortly with three others and all of us said our goodbyes to Sande. Our group headed for Inverquharity.

Chapter 10

It was a pleasant night for a ride. It was warmer than usual for a night in January, chilly but nowhere near freezing. There was a nearly full moon that gave us ample illumination for the trip home.

My father was driving the carriage and the Laird and his daughter were in the back. We rode along in silence for the first mile or two, the only sound to disturb the silence of the night being the horse's hooves striking the hard packed road.

I wanted to ask my father what his meeting with the abbot had been about but I didn't know how to go about doing that without appearing to pry. I was wondering how to bring the subject up when I was pleasantly surprised by my father asking, "Would you like to know what the abbot and I discussed tonight?"

"Yes, I would," I quickly replied.

"Well the abbot is not at all happy with the Justiciar, or rather the Justiciar's son. "

"Does the abbot know that Alexander Lindsay was behind today's raid?" I asked.

"He knows, he's not a stupid man. However knowing and proving are two different things. At any rate, the good abbot is thinking of replacing Lindsay with your uncle. He wanted to know what my feelings were about that."

"What did you tell him?"

"I told him that I didn't think the Lindsays would take to kindly to losing the position of Justiciar."

"But the abbot has the legal right to do that doesn't he?" I protested.

"Of course he does, but the Lindsays are not the type to worry about legal technicalities. I don't know how forceful their protest would be but I'm sure it would not be pleasant."

"Would Uncle Alexander even accept the Justiciar position now if it were offered to him?"

"Oh, I suppose he would," my father said. "My brother puts a great store in doing one's duty and I think he would feel honor bound to take the job."

"Why do you suppose Lindsay and his followers attacked the town today? Doesn't his father have a lot of money?" I inquired.

"Aye, his father has money but young Lindsay doesn't and I've heard he's heavily in debt. His father sent him to Paris last year to study but he didn't stay there very long. I've heard rumors that a man was murdered there and Alexander was the prime suspect. He was able to escape the hangman's noose, but in order to do so he had to pay a lot of money to a lot of people. That's why he is so much in debt."

"Can't he get his father to take care of his debt?"

"I don't think his father is exactly aware of what happened in Paris or the amount of debt his son owes. I also think Alexander doesn't want his father to know everything because he's afraid his father might disown him. Besides, I think young Lindsay and the band of cutthroats he associates with now would rather steal from people than come by their money in an honest way."

We spoke very little after that for the rest of the trip. The Laird and Ellene appeared to be asleep in the back of the carriage and my father appeared deep in thought. I too had many thoughts running through my mind, thinking of all that had transpired that day.

For the first time I had fought in a real battle and had experienced the wide range of emotions associated with combat. I had felt fear, anger, desperation, and sorrow. I also felt jubilation at having survived with the knowledge that I had acquitted myself well. May God forgive me, but I also felt some joy, or at least satisfaction at having killed a man in combat. It wasn't that I had a desire to kill someone or felt joy in killing, but rather that I had fulfilled my duty and in doing so had bought a guilty party to justice.

The other monumental occurrence that had transpired this day could be considered the polar opposite of being in combat; I had met a woman unlike any that I had ever met before. Images of our brief encounter; her smile, the soft touch of her hand, the sound of her voice and her beautiful face framed by lovely locks of blonde hair, kept going through my mind.

Violent images of the day's battle kept coming into my thoughts but they were quickly replaced with the soft and gentle remembrances of Ellene. I had never thought love at first sight was possible. I thought that was only something the poets wrote of and the bards sang about. However, I knew this night that I was hopelessly in love with Ellene, and I knew I had fallen in love with her the moment I saw her.

There were other thoughts that kept intruding on my consciousness that night. They were unpleasant and I tried not to think about them. I tried to push them out of my mind, but they were so repetitive and persistent that became impossible. These were thoughts of Alexander Lindsay. Each time I thought of him I felt a cold chill and wrapped my cloak tighter around my body. The cloak didn't help with that kind of chill though. Those chills came from way deep within my soul. I wondered if these thoughts were like a voice telling me to beware. However it wasn't just a voice, it was a scream that was warning me of danger.

Chapter 11

After arriving safely at Inverquharity, we unhooked the carriage and stabled our horses in the barn. Since it was late and getting colder, we invited our escorts to spend the night and they gratefully accepted our offer. I gave up my bedchamber so the laird and his daughter could have some privacy. I bedded down with the four guards by the fireplace in our main hall. The day's exertions were beginning to tell on me and within seconds of lying down I was sound asleep.

Since the main hall was just off the kitchen, the five of us awoke early the next morning to the sound of Besse preparing breakfast. We dressed quickly, as we were all anxious to get on the road back to Balmanoch to get our belongings. I especially wanted to get back to spend as much of the day with our visitors, especially the lovely

Ellene.

After a hearty breakfast of black pudding, eggs and porridge, we started out on our journey to Balmanoch. We got an early start. The sun was just showing above the horizon as we turned onto the main road. Since we had gotten off to such an early start, we decided to take a slight detour and go through Arbroath. We all wanted to see what the town looked like in the daylight after the previous day's destruction. We made good time and in a little more than two hours we had reached St. Vigeans church.

As we passed the church, I was struck by how much had transpired in the previous 24 hours. What had been a frantic race into Arbroath from this spot just a day earlier was now a pleasant ride with my friends. In fact, it was such a pleasant ride that the events of the day before were like a dream. It wasn't until we passed the burnt out buildings and saw the new caskets in front of the joiner's shop that I realized that my recollections of the previous day were indeed a reality.

The townsfolk were busily cleaning up from the fighting as well as from the festivities of the previous day and night. There were repairs already started on the buildings that had been damaged by fire that were repairable. There seemed to be only two structures that were beyond repair and debris from those buildings was being tossed into wagons and hauled away.

The area where I had killed my adversary and that had been so badly stained with blood had been raked and cleaned so that no evidence of the fight could be seen.

After surveying the scene of our battle, we turned around for the short ride to Balmanoch. We soon came to our camp and I was grateful that the first person I saw was my friend, Malcome.

"Hello, Malcome," I called out to him.

"Welcome back, Campbeel. Ah see ye survived yer trip haem. When Ah hud heard ye hud gain back haem lest nicht ah was afraid ye main hae rin intae some ay th' remnants ay Lindsays gang."

"We had a nice trip back. We didn't see any sign of Lindsay or his gang, but if we had, I'm sure my friends here would have been more than a match for them," I said, motioning towards my traveling companions. "How is Duncan this morning?" I asked a bit apprehensively, "I hope he's not holding any grudges from last night."

"Ah, Campbeel, Ah hink yoore in luck thaur. It seems uir mukker Duncan hud sae much tae drink lest nicht he doesnt membur a thin."

"Well that's a bit of good news," I said with a smile on my face. "I would not want a lad as big as Duncan to hold a grude against me."

We all walked into the barn we had used for our living quarters and I could see a lot of the fellows had already left. Duncan was sitting at the table by himself and I walked over to say hello.

"Hi, Duncan, Malcome told me you may have overdone it a bit last night."

"At ah did Campbeel. Ah hae a bad hangowre thes morn. In fact its sae bad e'en mah beak hurts, ne'er hud 'at happen afore," Duncan responded, sounding truly unhappy.

It was very difficult for me not to laugh, but the knowledge that it might go bad for me if I did helped me to control myself. Instead, I said in my most solicitous voice, "Sorry to hear that Duncan, especially the news about your sore nose. There must have been some bad ale you had last night."

"Yer probably reit. Ah weel hae tae be mair cannie in th' future."

After exchanging a few more pleasantries with Duncan, I quickly packed up my few belongings and tied them to my horse. I then went back to say my goodbyes.

As I was going back inside the barracks, a very stylish carriage with a driver pulled up. A very pretty lass in the back leaned forward and called out to me, "Would you please tell James I'm here for him?"

After assuring the lady I would give James the message, I went back into the barracks. I saw James as he was busy packing his belongings into a canvas bag and walked over to him.

"James, there's an attractive young woman in an expensive carriage out front looking for you. You best hurry along; I don't think she's one that likes being kept waiting."

"It's always good to keep them waiting for a while, Campbell. You don't want them taking you for granted," James replied with a big grin. In a more serious vein he said, "I guess I won't see you for a while so good luck, it's been nice training with you."

"Nice training with you as well," I replied. "Safe trip to wherever you're headed."

With that, James was off and I made the rounds saying goodbye to the many friends I'd made the past several months. Since most everyone there were from the county of Angus, I knew that I'd probably run into them again in the near future. However, it was still difficult parting company with lads that I'd lived and worked with for such a long time.

It was particularly difficult saying goodbye to Sande. I had learned so much from him the past while. His training is what had probably kept me alive in the fighting of the day before.

"Well, Sande, I'm off now," I began when I had a minute alone with him. "Thank you for all the training and for all you've done for me."

"I'm the one that should be thanking you," Sande responded. "You've become a fine warrior and I know that you and the others will serve our King and country well when the need arises. I'll look forward to working with you again in the spring." Sande embraced me and we all said our final goodbyes and left Balmanoch.

Malcome, Duncan and I left together since our homes all lay in the same general direction. Duncan rode with us nearly to Forfar where he turned off to where his family's estate was located.

After saying good-bye to Duncan, Malcome and I continued on our journey. It was shortly after noon, and we were nearly through the town of Forfar when we noticed a commotion ahead of us.

Two men, obviously drunk, were dragging an unfortunate woman out of a pub by her hair. I immediately recognized one of the men as one of the three that had accosted me in Dundee. The one that Sande had swatted with the side of his sword.

"Lemme go! Lemme go!" the women screamed as she frantically but unsuccessfully tried to break free of their grip.

"We'll teach ye tae insult an' overcharge us ye mucky-heap," one of the men said in a drunken brogue. "Tae settle th' scair we'll jist lit ye bestaw some ay yer feminine favors oan me an' mah mukker. Here now, I'll gie ye a little shogie bogie," he continued as he wrapped his arms tightly about the poor women before sliding one hand down to grab her in the groin area.

I quickly spurred my horse forward and reined in very close to the three of them. "Let her be," I commanded as my horse backed and snorted, sensing the anger and hostility of the two men and the fear of the women.

The man looked at me and released his grip on the women, who quickly ran sobbing back inside the pub. "Weel, weel," the man said as his eyes lit with recognition. "It's wee Ogilvy witoot th' protection ay his sodger friend," he continued as he and his associate quickly drew their swords and made ready to strike me.

I quickly realized I had made a mistake in confronting these men without first drawing my own weapon but I needn't have worried. Malcome, having quickly sussed out the situation had dismounted and walked up just behind and to the right of my attackers with his sword drawn.

Realizing the two meant to do me serious bodily harm, Malcome bought his sword down with both hands with as much force as he could muster. His blow struck the hilt of one of my adversary's sword with so much force it knocked it out of his hand and also severed his thumb at the base. The force of his swing continued on to cut deeply into the man's forearm.

Doubling over with a howl of pain and outrage, the surprised ruffian pressed his arm into his abdomen in an attempt to stop the blood which was now spurting from the stump of his thumb and the laceration on his forearm.

By this time, I had drawn my own sword and had the point of it pressed firmly into the neck of the other fellow. By lifting the sword just a bit, I made him stand on his tiptoes to keep the sword from cutting into his throat. I told him to drop his sword, which he quickly did.

"Yoo've made a big mistake, laddie. Dinnae ye ken wha we ur?" the man said with more than a touch of fear in his voice as my sword was still planted firmly in his neck.

"Yes, I know who you are. You're two drunken arseholes, one of which has just lost a thumb and who are both about to lose their heads if they don't get out of my sight immediately." With that, I drew back my sword and smacked him in the back of the head with the swords flat surface. "And take that with you," I told him as he fell to the ground.

After scrambling to his feet, he and his friend went to pick up their swords but I quickly cut them off. "Those swords don't belong to you anymore. The only things you're taking with you are your miserable lives, and you're lucky we're letting you keep them."

The two of them stumbled off, one holding his head and the other with his still bleeding right arm pressed tightly into his abdomen. As Malcome and I were picking up their swords the woman they had accosted came out of the pub.

"Thank ye genelmun so vera much," she began. "I dinna insult or overcharge em two ata. In fact, they dinna pay their charges and when they got so drunk they'uns did a lot of damage to me pub afore they turned on me."

"Glad we cud be ay service," Malcome replied.

"It was our pleasure," I added. "Since we have come into the possession of two swords that look to have considerable value let us pay you for the damages those two caused."

The lady protested that she didn't want any money from us but Malcome and I insisted, and in the end we paid her enough silver coins to cover her loss and the two of us continued on our way.

"Ye kent one ay those twa back thaur, didnt ye?" Malcome asked me before we had traveled very far.

"Aye, I know one of them. The tall bloke, the one whose thumb you cut off, is one of Lindsay's scoundrels, they probably both are. I've had trouble with that tall one before. He and Alexander Lindsay along with the man I killed yesterday attacked me in Dundee a long time ago. I wouldn't be surprised if they weren't with the group we chased out of Arbroath yesterday."

"Ah recon frae whit happend yesterday an' noo th-day Lindsay isnae thinkin' tae highly ay us reit noo."

"I'm sure he's not," I said laughing. Although I laughed at what Malcome had said, I also felt apprehension at hearing his words. I knew that Lindsay and his cronies would be eager to settle the score with us if they ever got the chance.

It was a short ride from Forfar to Malcome's family estate. We quickly arrived at the lane that led to their holdings. We said our goodbyes and parted, each of us taking one of the swords. I continued on my journey and arrived at Inverquharity shortly after noon.

Chapter 12

Thom walked out to meet me as I rode into our courtyard. "You made good time," he said.

"I made great time and even managed to rescue a damsel in distress on the way through Forfar," I replied before telling him the whole story about the run-in Malcome and I had had with the Lindsay cronies.

"I'm glad you made it back in one piece. There doesn't seem any end lately with the problems that Lindsay and his supporters are causing."

"No there isn't, and I'm afraid things will get even worse if young Lindsay becomes Justiciar," I replied as I unloaded my horse and handed the reins to Thom. "Would you give Malice a good rub down and an extra bit of grain? After all the traveling we've done the past two days, I think he's overdue for a rest."

"Aye, that I will. I'll take good care of him Mister Campbell," Thom answered.

I couldn't help but notice with a certain degree of pride that that was the first time Thom had called me Mister Campbell. Before that I had always been Master Campbell or just Campbell. My exploits of the previous day seemed to have elevated my standing.

As I walked inside the castle I was pleased to see that Ellene was the first person I saw. She was sitting in front of the fire and looked even more beautiful than she had the previous night. The smile she gave me as I walked into the room where she was sitting made my heart skip several beats.

"Hello, my Lady," I said, trying not to let my voice reveal the nervousness I was feeling. "Did you and your father sleep well?"

"We slept very well. That was very kind of you to give up your bed chamber for us. And, Campbell, my friends all call me Ellene and I want us to be friends." Ellene replied, flashing a row of beautiful white teeth.

"The pleasure was all mine… Ellene," I stammered. Quickly changing the subject, I asked "Where is your father?"

"Your father and mine went hunting first thing this morning. They haven't gotten back yet. It's given me a chance to have a nice visit with your mother and sister. I've had a very pleasant morning."

"I'm glad to hear that. If you don't have any plans would you like to accompany me on a walk about our estate?" I asked, hoping Ellene wouldn't notice the tremor in my voice or think I was being to forward.

"Aye, I would," Ellene replied. "I've been inside all morning. It would be nice to get out for a walk."

I felt like jumping for joy but managed to control my emotions and simply said, "Well let me put my belongings away and we'll be off." I quickly put the items away I had bought back from Balmanoch and returned to where Ellene was sitting. I helped her don her cloak and we set out together. She gently slipped her hand in the crook of my arm as we walked. Her hand looked so beautiful resting gently on my arm and the slight pressure of her hand made my spirits soar even higher.

We had a lovely walk. I showed her our animals: the cows, oxen, pigs, chickens, and sheep. She even stopped to pet one of the year old lambs that came up to us. I showed her the barns and storage sheds. We saw where our peasant farmers lived and then walked down to the burn that ran near the edge of our property.

It was a sunny day and the temperature was well above freezing but there were still icy patches along the edges of the water from the night before. The burn was about two feet wide at this point. I stepped across and offered Ellene my hand to help her over. She accepted my offer and stepped gracefully over.

I liked feeling Ellene's hand in mine so that even after she was safely across I kept holding it. I waited for her to take her hand back but I was pleasantly surprised that she kept her hand in mine.

We smiled at each other and continued walking hand in hand for several minutes. We walked a bit farther into the woods and stopped and looked at one another. There was an awkward silence and I was desperately trying to think of something to say. Ellene just smiled at me as she stood on her tiptoes and kissed me lightly on the lips.

I was surprised that she had kissed me but not so surprised that I didn't immediately kiss her back. This kiss was long and drawn out with our arms wrapped tightly around each other.

After we kissed we continued to hold each other, not saying anything. I could feel her breasts against my chest and feel the vibration of her heart beating. We started to kiss again when we heard my father's voice calling for us. We reluctantly parted and started back.

"Thank you for taking me for a walk," Ellene said as she put her hand back in the crook of my arm as we walked.

"Thank you for walking with me," I replied. "Maybe we can go for another walk tomorrow?"

"I'd love to Campbell but I'm afraid not. My father said we're starting for home in the morning."

"I'm sorry that you have to go so soon," I said with obvious disappointment in my voice.

"I am too. I've enjoyed our time together even though it's only been a short while. I hope we can see each other again sometime soon."

"I hope so too. Will your father be coming back this way anytime soon?"

"I think he has to be up this way around the first of April. If he does do you think your father and uncle would let us stay with you again?"

"Oh, I'm sure they would, I'll ask and see. In the meantime would it be alright if I called on you at Balanthrot?"

"I'd like that, Campbell, you're welcome to stop by anytime," Ellene said with a smile.

When we arrived back at the castle Thom and another man were dressing out a large stag that my father had killed. Next to the one they were working on there was another stag that Laird George had shot, the arrow still protruding from its side.

"There you are," Ellene's father said as we approached. "We were wondering where you two were. As you can see our hunting trip was quite successful, looks like fresh venison for our evening meal."

"Campbell has been showing me around their estate," Ellene said.

"Well, that was very nice of him."

"And I've invited Campbell to come for a visit," Ellene continued. "I hope that is alright with you Father."

"That's braw with me," her father responded with a knowing smile that caused me to blush. "Campbell is welcome to visit us anytime."

That evening was a very pleasant one. My uncle and aunt had gone to visit relatives so it was just my family, Ellene and her father. George and my father regaled us with the details of their hunt. They each gave full descriptions of how they were able to make their kills and about the even bigger ones that had gotten away.

Ellene and I sat side by side, occasionally holding each other's hand when no one was looking. Bessie cooked the venison to perfection and for once my mother didn't try to stop me when I had as much ale as my father.

In the morning, Laird George and Ellene left early. I stood and waved goodbye to them until their carriage was out of sight and I then began making my plans to travel to Balanthrot.

Chapter 13

The next few months flew by. I was traveling to Balanthrot as often as I could and Ellene and her father came to visit us twice during that spring and summer.

It was a very happy time, perhaps the happiest time of my life. Whenever Ellene and I were together we would go for long walks in the woods, both at Inverquharity and Balanthrot. In the evenings we would sit by the fire talking and laughing quietly with each other.

One day in summer, during one of the times Ellene and her father had come for a visit, we walked along the same burn where we had shared our first kiss. It was a beautiful day. The air was warm and gentle. There was just enough of a breeze to bring us the pungent smells of the evergreen trees that grew on the hills to the west of us.

We sat down on the forest floor on an area that was covered with a soft bed of moss. There was still some dew on the leaves and there was a large mallow plant next to us that was in full bloom, its pinkish-purple flowers looking radiant in the sunbeams filtering through the trees. Our backs were resting on an evergreen tree that had fallen over in a storm. The branches of the fallen tree still had foliage that gave us shade and a feeling of protection. It was like our own private world.

We sat there together. Ellene was cuddled into my side with my arm around her. Behind us we heard a pinecone slipping and falling through the branches until it landed with a soft thump on the moss covered floor of the forest.

It was very peaceful and still. Ellene turned her head slightly and looked deeply into my eyes. We began to kiss. First they were tender kisses, then more passionate. That was the day we became lovers. We touched, caressed and loved one another until we were both overcome with desire. Our bodies giving and receiving pleasure from each other until we reached heights of pleasure and intimacy I didn't know was possible.

We made love twice that day. The first time was so passionate to be almost brutal. We both let our passions take control of our bodies as we tore each other's clothes off. We quickly came together in a passionate embrace that almost instantly produced incredible waves of pleasure coursing through our bodies.

The second time we focused more on the journey than the destination. We took time to explore the bits and parts of our bodies.

The first time had been physically satisfying but the second was emotionally satisfying as well.

Afterwards we lay together on the soft moss, holding each other and listening to the sounds of the forest. We lay that way for a long while, neither of us wanting to say a word that could possibly break the mood of tranquility that held us both in its embrace.

As the sun began dipping toward the horizon, we both stirred at the same time, realizing it was time to head back to the castle. The air was starting to cool as we started back.

"I have to tell you something, Ellene," I said as we walked along.

"And what would that be, Campbell," Ellene asked with a smile in her voice.

"Well, I want you to know that I'm going to marry you."

"How kind of you to let me know that, Mister Campbell. Now, do I get a say in that at all."

"Of course you do," I replied smiling. "Will you marry me?" I asked, this time in a very serious tone.

Ellene stopped and looked up at me. "Are you serious, Campbell? You're not teasing me?"

"Aye that I am, I'm very serious."

"And why would you want to marry me?" she asked.

"You know the answer to that," I replied. "It's because I'm in love with you and I want to spend the rest of my life with you."

"You've only known me a few months. How can you be so sure you want to spend the rest of your life with me?"

"I've known that I wanted to marry you from the first moment I laid eyes on you. There's no one I'd rather be with than you, no one that makes me happier or more content. There's no question in my mind that you're the one that I want for my wife. Now tell me," I went on, "don't you feel the same way about me?"

"Oh, Campbell, I do. I just wanted to be sure that you really loved me. And yes! I will marry you! I will marry you!" Ellene exclaimed as she grabbed me around the neck and held me tight.

We kissed and embraced some more before resuming our walk. We walked arm in arm at first but when we came in sight of the castle we changed to a more formal stance with Ellene's hand on my arm.

We talked about when we should tell our parents and we decided that sooner rather than later would be best.

The following morning I asked George if I might have a word in private with him. He walked outside with me where I very nervously and formally asked him for his daughter's hand in marriage.

George was silent for a moment, thinking deeply.

"Do you love my daughter?" he finally asked.

"With all my heart and soul," I replied.

"Is it Ellene's wish to marry you?"

"It is, sir. That's what we both want."

"Are you able to care and provide for a wife?"

"Yes sir, I can. I give you my word on that."

To my great joy and relief, George then smiled and said, "Well in that case you have my blessing." He then embraced me and told me how happy he was to have me as a son.

Afterwards, Ellene and I together told my parents of our wishes. My father was very happy and gave both Ellene and myself bear hugs. My mother broke down and cried but said her tears were tears of happiness.

We were married less than two months later. Father Maclaren of our church in Kirremuir performed the ceremony. It was on the 14th of September in the year of our Lord 1444. We were in the middle of our harvest at that time and putting off the marriage for a few weeks would have made sense. However, Ellene had a birthday near the end of September and she didn't want to wait until she was eighteen to be married. According to Ellene, a woman that was unmarried at eighteen was an old maid, and she wanted to avoid that stigma.

It was a small but very nice ceremony. Ellene wore a white dress her mother had made for her. Her hair was in braids wrapped tightly around her head with flowers woven into the braids. Duncan and Malcome were in attendance along with James and a few other fellows I had trained with.

Ellene's youngest sister Margaret, a pretty lass of about 5 or 6, was our flower girl. She spread a mixture of rose and carnation petals down the center of the church as Ellene and her father walked together to join the minister and me at the altar. The Laird placed his daughter's hand in mine before, with a tear in his eye, he joined his wife on one of the pews.

Father Maclaren, who thankfully was sober that day, joined us together and pronounced us man and wife. I kissed Ellene before we turned and walked out of the church.

We were both so happy that day, looking forward to a long and happy life together. If we had only known what fate had in store for us we would not have been happy at all.

Chapter 14

We had received word a few months previously that Abbot Walter had decided not to appoint my uncle as Justiciar. His dislike for the Lindsays was outweighed by his desire to avoid trouble. We weren't happy with the abbot's decision, but we understood his reasons. We resigned ourselves to Alexander Lindsay eventually becoming Justiciar. It was only a few days after our happy ceremony took place that an entirely different kind of ceremony took place at the abbey in Arbroath.

At this ceremony, the good abbot presided over the transfer of the position of Jusitciar from David Lindsay to his son, Alexander, the new Master of Crawford. I heard it was a very somber affiar, not well attended by many of the townspeople. There were a few Douglases and some Lindsays. Of course, the riff raff and nar-dowells that had come to make up Alexander Lindsay's entourage were there in abundance.

I was told there were more than a few sniggers as Abbot Walter was giving the charge and obligation to young Lindsay. "You are hereby appointed to be Chief Justiciar, Bailie of Regality, throughout the domain of the monastery. The power contained in this appointment gives you the authority and obligation to dispense law and justice through the domain of the monastery and to provide its citizens safety and security from lawbreakers." Abbot Walter paused, and as he did so, he motioned to the monk who quickly brought him a small wooden box. The abbot carefully took the box and, once he had it secured in both hands, he continued, "This box contains holy relics of our beloved Saint Andrew, part of his left little finger and a few strands of his hair. Raise your right hand and place your left hand upon the box, Alexander Lindsay." Once Lindsay did as he was instructed, the abbot went on, "Do you accept the honor and obligations of this office and swear to uphold the law and protect the citizens within the domain of this monastery?"

"Aye, that I do, Abbot," replied Lindsay with a touch of sarcasm in his voice. This produced a few more muffled laughs from some of his followers.

And with that, as they say, the die was cast. For better or worse, the county of Angus was now under the rule and law of Alexander Lindsay, Master of Crawford. As the good citizens of Angus were soon to find out, it was to be for the worse, much worse.

However, for my new wife and me, all those events taking place in Arbroath seemed totally foreign and removed from our world. Oh, we heard stories about some of the outrageous behavior of the new Justiciar and his followers. There were drunken escapades, intimidation and thefts. However, the transgressions were relatively minor and Lindsay was careful to avoid antagonizing any of the more powerful clans. As long as Lindsay retained the backing of the Douglases, and didn't commit anything too egregious, it was easier for everyone to ignore what was happening. The general feeling was that Abbot Walter and the monks of Arbroath Abbey had created this problem so it was up to them to solve it.

At any rate, Ellene and I, along with everyone else at Inverquharity, were too busy to worry about Lindsay. We had our hands full with the harvest. It had been a good growing season, much better than the previous couple of years and all of our peasant farmers, from the villein's to the freemen were bringing in a bountiful crop.

Our grain bins were filling to capacity. The annual slaughter of the sheep and cattle was being carried out and great stores of firewood and peat were being stacked and made ready for the coming winter.

My days were filled with the work of helping my father and uncle in running the estate and the nights were filled with the joy of spending time with my beautiful wife.

It wasn't long before the harvest was in, the meats were curing and the first chill winds of winter were in the air. It was around this time that Ellene informed me that she would be making me a father sometime before the next summer. Life was good.

The time for our Harvest Day Celebration or Michaelmas was upon us and we made plans to go into Dundee for the Celebrations. Ellene's father had come for a visit and he traveled with us in his carriage along with my father and Ellene. My uncle and I rode our horses. Except for Ellene, we all carried swords. I even carried the axe I had used to such good effect when Lindsay and his cohorts attacked Arbroath.

The purplish Michaelmas daisies were blooming along much of the route into town. Once we entered Dundee, it was difficult to make any headway; there were so many people in the streets. I think everyone had had a good harvest and there was a lot to celebrate and for which to be thankful.

I was happy to see a lot of my friends from Balmanoch in town that day. Duncan, Malcome and James were there as well as a number of the other lads I had trained with. It was nice catching up with the lads I hadn't seen in many months.

James surprised us all by being in the company of a young woman named Violet whom he introduced as his wife. It was even more surprising that they had a child with them that he informed us was their first born. He was a cute little boy they had named Thomas who looked just like his father. None of us had been invited to his wedding, but when we asked him about it, James just said it was a small quiet affair with just immediate family present. I couldn't help but smile as the image of James being marched into the church with the business end of a drawn sword at his back flashed through my mind.

Everyone seemed to have a nice time that day. There were the usual acrobats and jugglers, and this year, there was even a fire eater and a sword swallower.

We enjoyed the entertainers and tossed them a few coins. Then after buying a few items from some of the many tradespeople that had set up stalls for the occasion, we retired to a respectable pub for a meal and a few rounds of ale.

Duncan and Malcome had joined my family at the pub and we enjoyed each other's company as well as the food and several pints of ale. After our meal, it was early evening so we decided to head back to Inverquharity.

It was as we were leaving the pub that my blood ran suddenly very cold. Across the street from us was Alexander Lindsay with a couple of his gang. He was staring at me until he realized that I was also looking directly at him and then he turned away. He and the two others walked away from us and then disappeared down the nearest close.

Malcome and Duncan had also seen Lindsay at the same time that I did.

"Weel that's a secht tae make a pleasent forenicht unpleasant," Duncan said referring to Lindsay.

"Wi' 'at cut-throat abit Ah wooldnt feel safe oan th' roads. Ah hink Duncan an' Ah shoods accompany ye oan yer way haem," Malcome added.

"Thank you for your offer but we'll be fine," I replied with a confidence I didn't truly feel. "There are three of us with swords so

I don't think we'll have any problem."

We said our goodbyes to everyone and then started on the long ride back to Inverquharity. My father was driving the carriage with George and his daughter in the back. I was riding next to the carriage and my uncle was bringing up the rear.

"We saw Lindsay as we were leaving the pub," I told my father when we had gone a few miles out of town.

"So that's what the three of you were talking about. I heard Malcome offer to ride back with us; maybe we should have taken him up on his offer," my father responded.

"Well now that Lindsay is our new Justiciar maybe that will cause him to be more respectable, besides, with all he and his crew have stolen, I'm sure his debt situation has improved," I replied.

"I hear he's still very heavily in debt, lots of gambling losses," my father said, before continuing in a rather hesitant voice. "There may also be another reason Lindsay acts the way he does. There's a story, and I'm not sure I believe it, but there's many who swear that it's true. The story is that Lindsay is controlled by the Devil himself, that the Devil owns his very soul."

"That sounds like something that comes out of a tavern when too many rounds of ale have been consumed," I said, laughing.

"It's much more than that," my father went on. "A number of years ago, Alexander Lindsay was playing cards at Glamis Castle with a group of his more respectable associates. It was on a Saturday and when the hour of midnight came no one would continue playing because it was now the Sabbath. No one that is except Lindsay.

He was drunk and insisted that everyone keep playing but no one would. He was quoted as saying 'I don't care what day it is; I'll play til doomsday with the Devil himself if I want.' It was shortly after he said that, there came a knock on the door. One of the servants answered it and there was a man no one knew dressed all in black. This man inquired if anyone wished to play cards, and Lindsay, staggering to his feet, invited the man in. They went to Lindsay's chamber and played cards all night. As the story goes the stranger was the Devil himself and he ended up taking Lindsay's soul. The story might not be true, but one thing that is true is that no title or position will ever make Lindsay respectable. He's a wicked man that has done many evil things. You never want to turn your back on him, not even for an instant."

I felt a chill run up my spine as my father concluded his story. I wasn't sure if I believed what he had told me, but I knew there was no question that Alexander Lindsay was a very dangerous person. I also knew that as long as he was around there would be more trouble.

We had continued on for another mile or two when I thought I heard a sound in the woods to my left. I dismissed it as just coming from an animal, but then I heard a louder sound that was closer to us. The sounds made me realize how vulnerable we were and I regretted not having the others to escort us back home.

A third sound, louder still, made me realize that there was definitely someone in the woods and he was keeping pace with us. The others also heard this sound and my uncle called out, "Who goes there? Who are you and what do you want?"

The answer we received was a quarrel shot from a crossbow that just missed my chest and slammed into the side of the carriage. My father raised his arms to slap the horse with the reins when a second quarrel sliced into the side of his neck. Blood came spurting from the wound and my father fell back dead in the carriage.

Horseman came pouring out of the woods and I drew my sword to attack but someone grabbed me from behind and pulled me off my horse. "Don't kill him, I want him alive," I heard a familiar voice say and my heart sank as I recognized the voice as belonging to Alexander Lindsay. "Tie him up and get the others out of the back of the carriage." I was gripped tightly and my arms were pulled roughly behind my back. I could feel my wrists being bound with rope, and out of the corner of my eye, I saw that my uncle was also on the ground with his hands bound behind his back.

To my horror, I could also see Laird George and Ellene being hauled roughly out of the carriage. George had not had time to draw his sword, but he still fought back valiantly. He struck one of his attackers with his fist which sent the man flying backwards. He drew back to strike another, but before he could follow through, Lindsay plunged his sword completely through his belly. The bloody end of the sword was protruding out of the Laird's back as he sank to his knees. Lindsay had a smile on his face as he thrust the heel of his boot against his victims shoulder and withdrew his sword. George fell over backward and was moaning softly when Lindsay thrust his sword through his body again, this time through his heart, killing him instantly.

Ellene broke away from a man that was holding her and knelt by her father's side. She was sobbing and calling her father's name when Lindsay grabbed her roughly by her hair and pulled her up. "Ah, what a pretty lass," Lindsay said as he pressed his bearded face close to hers. "It's a pity that I can't keep you alive; a wench like you would be nice to hump more than once. Unfortunately, due to the circumstances, I'm afraid that after my men and I are done with you tonight, we'll have to kill you," he said with an evil grin on his face. Looking in my direction, Lindsay continued. "We'll let your husband watch all the festivities before we kill him as well."

"Let her go, Lindsay," I said. "She hasn't harmed you at all."

"No, but you have, little Ogilvy. I always pay my debts and tonight is payback for the scar you gave me and also for my men that you and your group have killed and injured."

Lindsay turned back to Ellene and said, "Now my sweetheart let's start things off with a little kiss." However when Lindsay tried to kiss her, Ellene bit his lip and then spat in his face as he drew back. "You bitch," Lindsay roared and slapped Ellene so hard he knocked her senseless to the ground. He then bent over and ripped her dress down the front and began to raise the front of his kilt above his waist, exposing his fully erect manhood.

As this was taking place I noticed some movement at the back of the carriage. I stole a glance to the right and saw a familiar face glancing around the back wheel. Malcome had a reassuring smile on his face and he put his index finger to his lips to keep me quiet before ducking back behind the carriage again.

In order to buy time, I yelled at Lindsay "You say you always pay your debts but I heard that you're nothing but a deadbeat. I hear you can't pay your bills and that you're too cowardly to tell your father about it."

My outburst had the desired effect as Lindsay flew into a murderous rage and ran towards me. He tried to kick me in the head but I was able to roll out of the way and Lindsay's booted foot sailed harmlessly over me, just grazing the top of my hair. His miss caused him to lose his balance and as he stumbled I immediately threw my weight against his other leg, causing him to fall heavily to the ground.

I was wondering where Malcome was and if he was alone when the sudden movement of a well-aimed spear proved that Duncan was also in the vicinity. The tip of the spear struck one of Lindsay's men in the belly with such force it went completely through the man and the spear point lodged itself firmly into a tree that the unfortunate fellow was standing in front of. With the point stuck in the tree and the other end of the spear in the ground, the man's knees buckled but he could not fall to the ground as the spear held him up. He stayed that way, unable to move, as the blood poured out of him.

Malcome and Duncan now burst out from behind the wagon with swords drawn. Seeing his man spitted and held aloft by the spear and now seeing two armed men coming in his direction was enough for Lindsay. He quickly ran off into the woods.

The three that were left made an attempt to fight back. However Malcome quickly killed one with a savage swing from his claymore that opened him up from his shoulder to his hip. Duncan disarmed another one when that fellow tried lunging at him with a sword. Duncan simply stepped back and sideways and then cut the man's outstretched arm off at the elbow with a strong downward cut.

The third fellow, seeing how easily his friends had been dispatched, quickly threw down his sword and dropped to his knees, begging for mercy. A swift kick by Duncan to the side of his head sent him sprawling face down on the ground, and the point of Duncan's sword in the back of his neck kept him there.

Malcome quickly untied my uncle and me, and then I rushed to help Ellene, who was beginning to regain consciousness. I wrapped my cloak about her to hide her nakedness as I helped her get to her feet. Other than being badly shaken and having a large bruise on the side of her face where Lindsay had struck her, she appeared to be unharmed.

I led her away from where her father and mine lay dead to a fallen tree on the other side of the carriage. "Sit here Ellene, I'll be back in a minute," I told her. I was gratified to see that she didn't try and return to her father's body but instead sat quietly on the fallen log, sobbing softly.

I returned to where Duncan and Malcome were holding the two prisoners who were both sitting upright. They had tied a piece of rope around the stump of the man who had lost his arm and that seemed to have stopped the bleeding. I noticed they had also covered the bodies of my father and Laird George.

Seeing the two captives sitting next to the bodies of my father and George filled me with a murderous rage. I had my ax in my hand and I would have used it on them if Malcome had not grabbed my arm saying, "Control yerself, laddie. We need them alife tae testify against Lindsay."

"You're right," I replied as I put my axe away.

"Let's get Ellene back to Inverquharity," my uncle said. "I'll send some men with wagons back for the dead. I'll recruit some other men to join us and we can take the prisoners back to the abbey and report this crime. I don't care how powerful the Douglases are," my uncle continued, "this time the abbot can't ignore Lindsay's behavior." The anger in my uncle's voice was palpable.

We tied our captives onto their horses and tied the horse's reins onto the back of the carriage and set off for Inverquharity.

Chapter 15

It didn't take us long to get back to Inverquharity and for that I was thankful. Ellene was very distraught and I wanted to get her back home and into bed as soon as possible. She sat next to me as I drove the carriage and said nothing the entire trip. Her quiet sobbing the only sound she made as she tightly clutched my arm.

My concern for Ellene helped me with my own grief, which was overwhelming. I was all but numb from the shock of the evening's events. The knowledge that Ellene needed me now more than ever helped me to keep going.

My uncle was in the back of the carriage and Duncan and Malcome were riding behind to keep an eye on our captives. As we neared the castle, Duncan pulled alongside, "Fit like?" he asked with concern in his voice.

"We're fit thanks to you and Malcome," I replied." How did you two happen to show up when you did?"

"Ah, we saw Lindsay an' his cohort's follaw yer crew as ye went oot ay toon. We figured they waur up tae nae guid sae we tagged alang," Duncan explained.

"Well we're thankful you did. If you hadn't shown up we'd all be dead now."

"Was nae bother," Duncan responded. "Ah jist hope yer guid-wife will be awe rite."

"She'll be fine," I replied as I squeezed Ellene's hand tightly. I was grateful that Ellene squeezed my hand in return.

By this time we were home. My uncle set off to recruit help in retrieving the remains of the deceased and accompany us to Arbroath.

The prisoners were made secure. Aid was given to the man that had lost his arm. He had lost a lot of blood and was not doing at all well.

While the others were thus occupied, I took Ellene inside and sat her down by the fire. I then broke the news to my mother and Fiona, who were then as distraught as Ellene. I had never seen my mother as upset as she was that night. I had them all sit at a table by the fire. Besse brought them some food and her special concoction of warmed milk and honey mixed together with large amounts of whisky. Besse claimed her concoction would cure all ills, both physical and mental.

We sat for some time by the fire and I tried to answer the

questions that my mother and Fiona asked me as well as I could. I was relieved when my uncle came in the room to announce he had a group ready to travel to Arbroath. He told me I could stay if I wanted, but I needed to do something. Besse assured me she would take care of Ellene and the rest of my family. I set off with the others on a fresh horse that had been saddled and made ready for me.

There were about a dozen in our party. We left the injured prisoner, who told us his name was Rechard, with a guard and under the watchful gaze of Besse. The guard probably wasn't necessary due to the injured prisoners weakened condition, but we weren't taking any chances. The other prisoner we tied securely to his saddle and we set out to make our report to Abbot Walter.

It was well after midnight by the time we started off and starting to get cold. We had our cloaks wrapped tightly around us as we made our way slowly to Arbroath. I remember dozing off as we rode along. Others slept as well. One poor fellow actually fell out of his saddle and landed with a thump on the ground. Normally an incident like that would have caused a great deal of laughter but due to the somber mood, no one made a sound. We just waited until the lad had gotten to his horse and remounted. Then we continued our trip.

When we arrived at the abbey it was very early in the morning. The sun had still not risen and my uncle hesitated a moment as he stared at the abbot's quarters above the west gate, wondering if he should waken the abbot. He quickly decided the seriousness of the situation outweighed any need for concern about disturbing the abbot at such an early hour. He began to knock on the door. A tentative light knock at first, then banging much harder with his fist.

It took a couple of minutes before we saw any sign of anyone hearing us. Eventually though, we saw a light flickering from the window as the abbot or someone lit a candle. It took several minutes more before we heard a sleepy, irritated voice on the other side of the massive door asking us why we were causing such a racket at this time of night.

My uncle identified himself and apologized for the early hour, but said that he must speak with Abbot Walter immediately.

"And why must this conversation take place now and not at a more decent hour?" the voice on the other side of the door inquired.

My uncle hesitated, but only for a second before replying, "Because your Justiciar has committed murder this night and many more may die unless he is stopped."

There was silence for a few seconds and then we heard the bolt on the door being slid back and the creak of the hinges as the massive door slowly swung open. On the other side of the door we saw the abbot, standing between two large monks who were each holding a flaming torch. The abbot bowed slightly and motioned us to enter. When our entire group was inside the monks shut the massive door and bolted it.

"God bless you for seeing us at such an early hour, Abbot Walter," my uncle said.

"And may God bless you if this is not the life and death emergency you said it was," the abbot replied in a most peevish tone of voice. "You may follow me to my quarters, the rest of you stay here."

The abbot turned and headed back to his quarters, followed by my uncle and the two monks. We had not waited many minutes however before one of the monks returned. He asked me to take the prisoner, along with a couple of guards, in to see the abbot. I asked Duncan and Malcome to help me and the four of us followed the monk up the stairs to the abbot's quarters.

The sun was just beginning to show above the horizon by this time but it was still dark in the room we entered. There were a number of candles lit, and they helped somewhat, but the room was still dark and gloomy.

My uncle and the abbot were sitting at a table and the four of us stood in front of them. The abbot asked me to tell what had happened which I did. The abbot then asked our prisoner, a man of about 30 whose name was Silas, to tell us what happened.

Silas refused to talk, other than to say he would only answer to the Justiciar. Upon hearing Silas's refusal to talk, Malcome put his knife to his throat and told him, "Laddie, either yer words ur yer guts ur comin' ot. Th' choice is yers."

Silas's bravado vanished under Malcome's threat and he plaintively said, "Ifn I tell yu anything Lindsay'll kill me fur sure."

"Mebbe he will an' mebbe he willnae. Th' only thin' fur certain is 'at if ye dornt gab noo weel kill ye fur sure," was Malcome's unsympathetic reply as he pushed his knife deeper into Silas's neck, drawing blood.

That was enough encouragement for poor Silas and he answered all the abbot's questions, confirming the events of the previous night. The only difference was he told us he was an unwilling participant, forced by Lindsay to go along with it. Of course no one believed him.

The abbot then excused us and the four of us left to wait outside with the others. A few minutes more and my uncle joined us.

"What did the abbot say," I inquired.

"He's furious. He's immediately calling a meeting of all the monks to determine what they're going to do. He's asked us to stay for a few hours until they meet. He said we could get some sleep in the monk's quarters until their meeting is over."

A few hours' sleep is what we all needed, so we gratefully followed a monk to where they resided. Our guide took us to a building at the back of the abbey. When we entered the building we found ourselves in a large room filled with tables and benches. We walked through that room into a hallway with rooms on either side. Each of these rooms contained two wooden beds covered with a thick blanket of straw. The monks were all awake by this time and our guide told us we could sleep wherever we pleased. Duncan and I were right behind the monk and we walked into the first room we came to. We each took a bed and were asleep in seconds.

Chapter 16

It was well past noon when we were awakened by an elderly monk. "The abbot wishes to see you at your earliest convenience," the monk intoned before bowing and withdrawing from the room. As we brushed the straw from our clothes, we heard the monk awakening the others.

As we walked out of the sleeping area into the large room with the tables and benches, we were surprised and delighted to see the monks had prepared a meal for us. The food could not have come at a better time, as we were all ravenous, not having eaten since the day before.

It was actually quite a feast. They had bread and cheese with plenty of ale to wash it down. There was some dried fish and even a bit of haggis. We all ate our fill and when we were finished the same elderly monk who had awakened us came to escort us to the abbot. At first I thought he just wanted my uncle to follow him, but he made it clear that we were all expected to come.

The monk led us to the same room as we had been in previously. The abbot was sitting at a long table with three of his monks on either side. The monks all rose and bowed slightly as we entered the room. There were benches set out in front of the monks table and the abbot motioned for us all to sit.

After we had found our seats, the abbot rose and faced my uncle. "Alexander Ogilvy," the abbot began quite formally as he read from a parchment. "We, the monks of Arbroath Abbey, having been granted the authority to provide for justice, peace and tranquility for the citizens of Angus by Almighty God and King James, and that justice, peace and tranquility not being provided for by the current Justiciar, and the current Justiciar's conduct proving itself uneasy to the convent, immediately withdraw the position of Justiciar from Alexander Lindsay, otherwise known as the Master of Crawford, and hereby appoint Alexander Ogilvy of Inverquharity as Justiciar of Angus." Then looking at Uncle Alexander, the abbot asked, "Do you accept this appointment?"

My uncle looked stunned and didn't move for a few seconds. Coming to his senses, he then rose and addressed the monks. "I gratefully accept this appointment and with the help of Almighty God and the good King James will do my upmost to provide the protection of the law to the good citizens of Angus that they so richly deserve."

The abbot smiled at my uncle and said, "Then please raise your right hand and place your left hand on the Holy Relic of Saint Andrew to receive the charge." As the abbot finished speaking, the elderly monk hurriedly rushed over with the wooden box that was said to contain the relics of the beloved saint for my uncle to place his hand upon.

"Alexander Ogilvy," the abbot began. "Do you solemnly swear to uphold the law, dispense justice, and to the best of your ability, protect the populace of Angus from lawbreakers and evil doers?"

"I do," replied my uncle.

"Do you further swear allegiance to God, the King, and the monks of Arbroath Abbey?"

"I do."

"Then with those assurances, by the power granted me by God above through his humble servant, King James, I pronounce you Justiciar of Angus." With that, the abbot walked over to my uncle and embraced him as the rest of us applauded loudly.

"Thank you Abbot Walter, God willing I will bring the rule of law to Angus."

"I'm confident you will," replied the abbot.

The abbot then had all the members of our group sign, as witnesses, the proclamation that had made Uncle Alexander the Justiciar. Some of the fellows couldn't write and just made their mark. I didn't realize it at the time but those signatures and marks were to make the authors of them wanted men in the near future. It was easy for the monks to elect my uncle Justiciar; giving him peaceable possession of the position was to prove another matter altogether.

"With your permission," my uncle said, "I would like to begin my duties immediately."

"By all means," the abbot replied.

"In that case, I would like to bring the prisoner Silas to trial. Once he's had his fair trial, we can then take him out and hang him."

"You must do what you feel is just and fair," Abbot Walter replied.

"Then with your permission, I would appreciate the use of the dining hall to hold our trial."

"Granted, and if there is anything else you need all you have to do is ask."

"There is one more thing," my uncle continued. "I would like to issue a warrant for the arrest of Alexander Lindsay for the crimes of murder."

The abbot looked a bit taken aback at this request, but he quickly recovered and said hesitantly, "Yes, of course, that must be done."

"Thank you," my uncle replied. Turning to me, he said "Campbell, have the men assemble in the dining hall and have the prisoner Silas taken there as well."

Nodding my head in agreement, I quickly left the room, motioning for the others to follow. Having heard my uncle's words, some of the others had already run ahead and were bringing Silas into the dining hall at the same time as I was entering.

Silas's hands were still securely tied behind his back. He could not have known his trial was about to start, but the fear in his eyes showed that he knew something was afoot and whatever that something was would probably not be in his best interest.

By the time my uncle entered the dining hall, we were all seated on the benches. Striding to the front of the room, my uncle turned towards us and had a table and bench brought forward. Sitting on the bench behind the table, he motioned for a monk that had accompanied us to sit next to him. The monk had parchment, a quill, and an ink pot with him.

My uncle had obtained a wooden mallet to use as a gavel and he now banged the mallet loudly against the table. The monk, who was seated to my uncles left, immediately stood. The rest of us, taking our cue from the monk, also rose.

"This official court of the County of Angus is now in session," my uncle said in an authoritative voice. "Be seated."

"Campbell, bring the prisoner forward and have him sit there." As he spoke, my uncle motioned towards a chair that had been placed just to the right of my uncle and in between my uncle's table and where the rest of us were sitting.

After Silas was seated my uncle turned towards him and said, "State your name for the court record."

"My nam is Silas Spink an' ye aint got noo reit tae treat me thes way," Silas responded with more than a touch of defiance in his voice. "My mukker Alexander Lindsay, he's th' law in Angus, an' ye can't dae nothin withit his say so."

"Your friend Alexander Lindsay is no longer Justiciar," my uncle replied." I'm the new Justiciar and in fact, your friend is a wanted man. Wanted for murder, same as you. If you're found guilty, we'll hang you. Do you understand these charges and what will happen if you're found guilty of them?"

My uncle's words seemed to take the wind out of Silas's sail. He nodded his head slightly to show that he understood the charges and then slumped down in his seat, staring at the floor.

"Campbell," my uncle continued, "Are there any witnesses to the crime that Silas is charged with?"

"Aye, I'm a witness, as are Duncan and Malcome, and you as well."

"Well, I'm the judge, so I can't testify, but you and the others can. Tell us what happened last night."

We all related what we had seen the night before, the monk seated next to my uncle scribbled furiously to take down all the testimony. After the last one of us had finished, Uncle Alexander asked Silas if he had any witnesses.

"Ye ken bludy weel Ah dornt hae onie witness but ah didn't kill nobody. It was Lindsay 'at did aw th' killin'" Silas replied.

"In that case, after hearing all the testimony this court finds you guilty as charged. The sentence is death by hanging and is to be carried out immediately."

"Nae! nae! Ye cannae dae thes," Silas blurted out.

Ignoring Silas's pleas, my uncle turned to me and said, "Campbell, you and the others take the prisoner outside and see that the sentence is carried out. The monks don't want a hanging to take place here in the abbey so take him into town, somewhere on the

High street and hang him there. It will be good for the public to witness the hanging. It will serve as a warning to other would be law breakers."

"At leest lit me write a letter tae mah mum," Silas continued to plead.

"I'll give you as much time to write letters as you gave my brother and Laird George," my uncle replied. "Take him outside and carry the sentence out, I want to be home before dark."

Duncan and one of the other fellows picked Silas up, one on either arm. They took him, half walking, half dragging, outside the abbey gates and onto the High Street.

We stopped in front of an ale house, not too far from the abbey. This ale house had a stable behind it. Above the first room of the ale house there was a loft area that was used to store straw and hay for the stable. The loft was accessible by a large door that was above the doorway to the ale house. Above this large door was a stout timber with a rope and pulley attached to it. The proprietor used this apparatus to raise the bales of straw and hay from the farmers wagons into his loft.

Judging this a suitable place to carry out the hanging, my uncle and I went inside to see the proprietor, a tall elderly gentleman with a long dirty beard. After explaining what we wanted, and paying him a few silver coins, the proprietor agreed to let us use his rope and pulley for the hanging. The proprietor was only too happy to oblige us since he knew a hanging taking place on his premises would be good for business.

We quickly fashioned a noose out of one end of the rope and pushed Silas forward. A large crowd had gathered by the time we had Silas positioned where we wanted him and the noose placed securely around his neck. His mouth opened a number of times, as if he was trying to speak, but no words came out. His eyes were wide with fear.

At a nod from my uncle, the rope was hauled down and the prisoner was jerked roughly upward. Silas's arms were tied tightly behind him but his legs were unbound and he kicked violently as he was lifted off the ground. The pull of the rope didn't snap his neck so Silas continued to twist and kick. His face turned red and then a deep purple and his eyes bulged gruesomely out of their sockets as the rope cut deeply into his neck. Yellow liquid ran down his legs as his bladder emptied. His torment continued for a good 10 minutes, until his struggles stopped. The now lifeless body hung motionless, the neck canted at a crazy angle with blood coming from the eyes, nose and ears.

"Our work is done here," my uncle said as soon as the body stopped twitching. "Time to head for home. We might even have time for another trial and hanging before the sun sets," he continued with more than a touch of relish in his voice.

We left poor Silas that way. I guess someone eventually came to dispose of the body but I never did hear what happened to it. Someone told me the proprietor left the remains hanging there quite a while since they brought in some curious customers. I was told it wasn't until the odor became offensive, that the body was cut down and disposed of.

Chapter 17

The ride back to Inverquharity was uneventful. We even arrived back with enough time to have another trial and hanging, but the Grim Reaper had beaten us to it. By the time we had arrived home, Silas's accomplice had succumbed to his injuries and was quite dead.

Ellene was still distraught. Her father's funeral was to be tomorrow at their family church in Perth. My father's was to be held the following day in the same church Ellene and I had been married in just a short while ago.

I related the events of what had happened in Arbroath. My mother, Fiona and Ellene all seemed thankful that Uncle Alexander had been made the new Justiciar. They were also thankful that justice had been dispensed to one of our attackers. There was still sadness in all their eyes that I knew would be there for quite some time. I also knew that until Alexander Lindsay was apprehended and brought to justice, we wouldn't be safe.

The next two days were cloudy and cold with intermittent rain. The dreich weather fit the somberness of the occasion perfectly. Both of the funerals went well, or at least as well as those types of melancholy ceremonies can be expected to go. Father Maclaren was drunk, as I expected, since my father's funeral wasn't held until late in the day, but fortunately not so drunk that it caused any real problems. I was gratified that Ellene, as well as my mother and sister, managed to get through both services without seeming to suffer any ill effects or worsening of the depression they were already dealing with.

It was after my father's funeral that Uncle Alexander rode his horse next to mine as we were making our way back from the church. "What do you think our next step should be, Campbell?" he asked me. "We must apprehend Lindsay, but I'm not sure how to go about doing that, at least not without starting a war with his family and the Douglases."

I thought for a long while before replying. I was flattered that my uncle thought enough of my judgment that he would seek my advice, but I knew there was no easy answer to that question. "I think the best thing to do is to send someone to meet with Lindsay's father," I suggested. "Tell him his son needs to come in and talk with you as part of an investigation into a crime that took place recently. David Lindsay has always been an honorable and decent man. If he's approached the right way, he might help us." The rain that had been just a slight drizzle now began to fall harder as I finished speaking.

My uncle was considering my suggestion when our attention was turned to a rider approaching us at a rapid pace. As he came near us, he slowed and then stopped his horse in front of my uncle. I recognized him as one of the monks from the abbey and from the lathered condition of his horse, it was evident he had ridden hard all the way from Arbroath.

"Laird Ogilvy," the monk began in a breathless voice, "Abbot Walter sent me. Alexander Lindsay and a group of about 20 armed men are at the gates of the abbey. They're threatening to burn the town down unless Abbot Walter renounces you as Justiciar and reinstates Lindsay."

Without a moment's hesitation, my uncle replied to the monk, "Tell the abbot that I'll raise as many men as I can and be there as soon as I can. I should be there late tomorrow morning." Then turning to me he said "Gather as many men as you can. Tell them what the situation is and to be ready to ride at dawn. I'm riding to Castle Ruthven to ask Sande's father, Lord Gordon, for his help."

Sande's father, the Earl of Huntly, Lord of Badenoch, Gordon, Strathbogie and Cluny, was a powerful chieftain. He was known to his friends as the "Cock of the North." He and my uncle had entered into a bond to defend one another if either was threatened.

"Would it help if Sande went with you? I'm sure he'd be willing to if you asked," I suggested.

"I don't think relations between Sande and his father are good right now," my uncle replied. "I think it's best if I go alone. I hope to be back at Inverquharity before dawn, with as many men as possible. And, Campbell," my uncle continued, "your idea to contact David Lindsay is a good one. Pick someone you trust to ride to Finavon castle to see Lindsay and explain what is happening and ask for his help. Also, talk with everyone at Inverquharity and as many of our neighbors as you can. Tell them we need their help and ask them to be at Inverquharity at dawn ready to ride with us to Arbroath." With that, my uncle turned his horse and started off at a fast clip towards Ruthven. The monk had already started back to Arbroath to deliver my uncle's message to the abbot.

After explaining what was happening to my mother and Ellene, I quickly kicked my horse into a gallop and headed back towards Inverquharity. Duncan and Malcome had both attended my father's service, but had left before we did. Since their lands were on the way to Inverquharity, I stopped to see them first and was fortunate to catch them both at home.

I came to Duncan's lands first and gave him the news. He quickly agreed to be at Inverquharity in the morning with as many men as he could muster.

I then stopped to see Malcome and asked him to deliver the message from my uncle to David Lindsay. Malcome was reluctant at first to do as I asked, wanting instead to accompany our group to Arbroath. However, after I stressed the importance of the message, he reluctantly agreed to leave for Finavon castle first thing in the morning. Malcome also agreed to contact as many men as possible before he left and have them muster at Inverquharity at dawn.

After arriving back home, I quickly spread the alarm among our villen farmworkers, and some lesser Lairds that owned small farms near our own. Almost to a man, they all agreed to assemble in the morning for the march to Arbroath.

Our villeins and neighbors were obligated to lend their support in an emergency. (The tenants, due to the terms of their contract and the neighbors, due to bonds they had entered into with the Ogilvys.) However, both groups showed genuine enthusiasm for our cause which far surpassed any legal obligation they had. I wasn't sure if the enthusiasm was because of their respect for my uncle or for their general dislike of Alexander Lindsay. Whatever the reason, I was grateful for the strong show of support.

By the time I returned home it was after dark. After making sure Ellene, my mother and sister were doing okay, I quickly ate, laid out the weapons and gear I would be taking with me in the morning, and went to my bed early. I knew that tomorrow would be a long day.

Chapter 18

It was still dark when I awoke and quickly dressed. By the time I went outside, dawn was breaking and the front of Inverquharity had close to 50 men readying for the trip to Arbroath. By the time the sun was fully over the horizon, my uncle had returned with Lord Gordon and an additional 60 men that swelled our force to over 100 strong.

Although Lord Gordon was resplendent in full battle dress, as were many others in his entourage, our group consisted of mostly farmers and a few fishermen. Very few of them had had any military training. Everyone had swords, although some were ancient and rusty. Most of us carried shields of some sort. About half also had a secondary weapon such as an axe or spear. Our spirits were high as we set off for Arbroath. What we lacked in training we made up for in enthusiasm.

The air was crisp and cool when we started. It had been unusually cold for early October and there were patches of ice along the sides of the burns and ponds we passed. It warmed up a bit as the morning wore on. In a short while, the warmer temperatures along with the exertion and excitement caused us to open our cloaks to get some relief from the heat.

It was nearly noon by the time the spires of the abbey came into view. We were soon on the high street which was mostly deserted except for two men I recognized as men I'd seen with young Lindsay. The rest of Lindsay's group was in the same ale house that we had hung Silas in front of just a few days before. I couldn't help thinking how appropriate it would be if Lindsay was given the same treatment on the same spot as Silas.

Lindsay's two men started for the ale house as soon as they saw us. Fortunately, by the time they had seen us some of our group was between them and the pub. We quickly surrounded the men and made them prisoner so that they were unable to alert Lindsay and his gang that we had arrived. Duncan pointed his sword at their necks and told them, "Any soond oot ay ye twa an' nae weel split ye frae yer beak tae yer nuts." The fear on their faces made me confident they wouldn't try to raise an alarm.

We quickly dismounted and Uncle Alexander told our group to follow him. The rest were to stay outside with the horses and guard the prisoners. We then drew our swords. With Uncle Alexander leading the way, our band strode purposely into the ale house.

The inside was very dim. The only light coming from the doorway and one small window to the right. It took a while for our eyes to adjust to the dimness but we soon saw that Lindsay and his men were congregated at the back of the pub. They were in front of a long plank sitting on top of two barrels that served as the bar. The only other furnishings in the building were a few stools and makeshift tables scattered around the room.

The first person to see us was the proprietor whose name we found out later was Thomas. He was still wearing the same dirty blouse and kilt that he was wearing when I saw him on the day of the hanging. Seeing a band of men with drawn swords gave him quite a fright and he quickly turned around and left the building by the back door.

As Thomas was beating a hasty exit from his ale house, some of Lindsay's men, most of whom already appeared quite drunk even though it was barely after noon, began to notice us. One poor fellow, a heavy set chap with red hair, made the unfortunate decision to draw his sword and attack us. He had taken barely a step in our direction when a number of our men were on him. He was quickly hacked and stabbed numerous times. He soon collapsed on the floor with blood gushing from numerous injuries and his entrails spilling out from a grievous wound to his abdomen.

Seeing the results of resisting us, the rest of Lindsay's men quickly threw down their swords and raised their hands in surrender. Lindsay was the last to drop his sword. For a second I thought he would come at us, but his keen sense of self-preservation kicked in and he wisely dropped his sword on the floor with the others.

"You are all under arrest," my uncle stated in a calm, matter of fact voice. "Outside! All of you."

"Uncle, let's get a rope and string Lindsay up, the others can wait but let's take care of Lindsay while we have him."

"No, Campbell," my uncle replied. "We'll go by the law. We'll give Lindsay his fair trial and then hang him."

My initial reaction to what I considered an unjust delay of justice was an urge to take the law into my own hands and cut Lindsay down with my sword on the spot. The fact that I didn't is one of my big regrets in life. So much hardship, death and destruction could have been averted if I had used my sword as I wanted to that day. I think I knew instinctively that a scoundrel like Lindsay would be too slippery to be brought to justice through any civilized means.

I think my uncle could sense my feelings because he went on to say, "We'll have the trial today, Campbell. Better to do it the right way rather than take the law into our own hands."

There wouldn't have been a long delay in order to have a trial and then "legal" hanging but it proved to be long enough for Lindsay to escape the noose. In less than an hour, we had asked for and received Abbot Walter's permission to again use the monks dining hall for a courtroom and were in the process of bringing all the prisoners inside when it was reported that three riders were riding hard into town.

I went out to see who was coming and saw that it was Malcome, David Lindsay and a third person I didn't recognize. As the three riders came to a halt and began to dismount I saw that this third person was quite well dressed and very young. He also had Grouse feathers protruding from the side of his hat, denoting him as the chieftain of a clan.

"Hello, William Douglas," my uncle's voice rang out from behind me. "And hello to you as well David Lindsay."

I had heard much about William Douglas, chieftain of clan Douglas, but I had never laid eyes on him before. I was surprised that someone so powerful was so young.

"Alexander," David Lindsay said as he nodded to my uncle in greeting and then asked, "Are you holding my son prisoner?"

"I am," my uncle responded. "I'm sorry, David, but your son has committed some heinous crimes and he must answer for them."

Lindsay didn't respond, but Douglas spoke sharply saying, "Release Alexander Lindsay at once, along with anyone else you're holding. You have no authority to act as Justiciar. If the monks wish to remove Alexander Lindsay as Justiciar, the position automatically goes back to his father, David Lindsay."

"My authority to be Justiciar comes from King James himself acting through his representative Abbot Walter."

"King James does not rule in Scotland. Those of you who wish to pretend he is king are free to do so but I don't recognize him as king nor does any other true Scotsman."

"You're the one who is pretending, Douglas. Whether you or anyone else likes it or not James has been recognized as the true and lawful king of Scotland. Now you'll have to excuse me, I have a trial to attend to."

"There will be no trial, Alexander."

"And how do you propose to stop us?"

"I have nearly 300 armed men that will be here in a few minutes. I had them start out a half-hour after we did so that we could have a reasonable discussion and peaceful settlement of this situation. I sincerely hope to settle this peacefully but if you will not be reasonable then we will have to resort to an arbitrament of the sword."

Almost on cue a dust cloud of immense proportions could be seen on the horizon, giving proof that a large number of horsemen were riding hard in this direction.

"Then so be it, William" my uncle said defiantly. "If it's an arbitrament of the sword you want then you shall have it. We'll kill half your force and the other half we'll try for armed insurrection against the crown. Then you and they can all hang together next to Alexander Lindsay."

I don't think Douglas was expecting that defiance nor do I think he was aware of the large number of armed men we had. His face didn't show any fear but it did show surprise and he didn't respond to what Uncle Alexander said. As more and more of our men began to appear on the street I think it began to dawn on Douglas that he may be in for more of a fight than he had thought.

By this time, Douglas' force began to come into town. I could tell he had nowhere near the 300 men he had boasted about but he still had more men than we had.

Without waiting to be told, I had our strongest and best men form a line from one side of the street to the other and put their shields together, one against the other. A lot of our men had had little or no military training but with the help of Duncan and Malcome and a couple of others that had trained with us we got them into a tight line. Each end of our line ended against a building so we couldn't be flanked.

Our shield wall thus formed, I had a second row of men stand behind the men holding the shields. This second row were all armed with spears and were ready to help repulse any attack by shoving or throwing their spears over and between the heads of the men in the first row. The rest of our men, except for a handful that stayed back to guard the prisoners, filled in behind the first two rows. For a bunch of fishermen and farmers, I thought our formation looked quite good and formidable.

"Stop! Gentleman," David Lindsay suddenly interjected. "Let's act like civilized men and settle this without bloodshed." Turning to my uncle he continued, "Nothing can be gained by killing one another. If my son has committed these crimes you say he has, then he and any accomplises should be brought to trial.

"All I ask is that any trials wait until after it's decided by an appeal to the council of all the clan chieftains of Angus who is the rightful Justiciar of Angus. I know you feel you are the rightful Justiciar, but I also have what I feel is a legitimate claim to that office. If it is decided that you are the Justiciar of Angus, then the trial may proceed as you wish. If it's decided I'm the Justiciar I'll still have the trial, and in the interests of fairness, I'll allow the trial to be presided over by one of the Justiciars of a neighboring county. In the meantime, as long as I have your word no harm will come to my son, he may remain in your custody. What say you to that, Alexander Ogilvy?"

I personally would have rather had it out with them then and there but I knew my uncle couldn't do that. Lindsay's offer, as much as I hated to admit it, was fair. It would avoid a lot of bloodshed, and I felt the clan chieftains would side with my uncle. In addition to his being appointed Justiciar of Angus by Abbot Walter, my uncle had a heredity claim to that position; all the Justiciars of Angus had been Ogilvys for many generations. However, even if the post went to Lindsay, he had promised to still have his son tried for his crimes with an independent judge. David Lindsay was an honorable man that could be trusted. His son remaining in our custody would help to insure against any unpleasant surprises.

My uncle thought about Lindsay's proposal for a long moment but in the end he did what he had to do. He accepted Lindsay's offer in its entirety. The three men embraced, ending the stand-off. The crisis now being over, the men on both sides relaxed and headed for home.

It was a good, well thought out agreement and it was fair. Unfortunately like so many good, fair, well thought out agreements, it quickly unraveled.

Chapter 19

David Lindsay asked to see his son before he left and Uncle Alexander granted his request. We led him to where his son and the others were being detained so David could have several minutes alone with his son. After their conversation, I was pleased to see that judging from the angry expression on his face, young Lindsay was quite unhappy with the arrangements.

After David left, we went to see the abbot, who was obviously relieved that there had been no bloodshed or damage done to the abbey or Arbroath itself. We explained the agreement we had made with Lindsay and Douglas and asked if the abbot could keep Alexander Lindsay in custody until the council had met and made their decision.

The abbot quickly agreed, knowing there really weren't any

suitable structures in the vicinity to securely keep anyone captive. The abbot was also astute enough to realize that as long as Lindsay was held captive everyone would be safer.

"We can keep young Lindsay in the sacristy. It's pleasant enough for an extended stay and quite secure," said Abbot Walter.

After getting vows from Lindsay's cohorts that they wouldn't take up arms against us or try to aid Lindsay in any way, we told them they were free to go. Vows from scoundrels such as those were, of course, quite worthless, but we couldn't keep them all prisoner and without Lindsay causing trouble the rest of them were probably harmless.

After making sure Lindsay was safely and securely ensconced in the sacristy, our group disbanded and headed for home. There was little to do now, but wait until we heard from the council. I busied myself with farm work and wondered when we would hear something.

Scarcely a week had gone by when a monk arrived at Inverquharity from the abbey. It was the same elderly monk we had seen before and from the looks of his lathered horse and his mud splattered robe it was evident he had ridden in much haste. I was gratified that he asked to speak to the Justiciar instead of Laird Ogilvy.

We quickly took him to my uncle. In a rather breathless voice he informed my uncle that the council had agreed to hear and mediate the disagreement between the Douglas-Lindsay faction and ourselves. The hearing was to be in two weeks hence, November 1st,

1444, at Glamis Castle. The fact that Glamis castle was owned by a member of the Douglas clan gave us some concern. However, since all the clan chieftains of Angus would be there, we felt my uncle would still have a fair hearing.

We awoke early on the morning of the first. We had about an hour's ride to Glamis Castle. We left much earlier than we had to, to allow for any delays. There were eight of us in total. Duncan and Malcome, along with four of our villein farmers, accompanied my uncle and me. It was a large enough group to provide for some security if things got out of hand, but not large enough to appear threatening.

The council meeting was to be just after the noon time meal. We arrived well before the appointed time. A large crowd had already gathered in the courtyard of the castle, waiting to be let inside. Counting all the chieftains and their attendants there must have been over 50 people milling about. Most of the people I didn't recognize. I did see David Lindsay and William Douglas along with a handful of others I had met on visits they had made to Inverquharity. There were a few others that I had seen at the funerals of my father and Ellene's father

A few minutes before the appointed time, the massive doors of the castle opened and we were ushered inside. There were a large number of servants that were taking everyone's weapons before they were allowed into the main part of the castle. Some objected to being disarmed, but it was a sensible precaution to take considering the strong feelings among many in attendance.

The castle was impressive. The Great Room in which we were to have the hearing was enormous and ornate. The walls were covered with large beautiful tapestries depicting hunting scenes, famous battles and royal ceremonies. The rug was thick and plush and looked to have been imported from the Far East. The parts of walls not covered with tapestries were adorned with portraits of past kings of Scotland and famous Douglases. Noticeably absent though were pictures of the current King James II, as well as his father, King James I.

Chairs were brought in to accommodate all those in attendance. There were sixteen clan chieftains or their lawful representatives in attendance. They represented all the major land holders in Angus. A long table facing the assembly was provided. My uncle and David Lindsay sat at this table on either side of the chieftain of the Erskine clan. The chief of the Erskine clan, whose given name was Patrick, was chosen by my uncle and Lindsay to run the council meeting. He was also the one who would oversee the vote that would decide who would be Justiciar. Erskine was chosen because of his reputation for honesty and integrity and because he had no alliances with either the Douglas-Lindsay clans or the Ogilvys.

Those in attendance seemed to be in an almost festive mood. Many of them had friendships that stretched back many years. There were even some that had faced each other in battle during some of the petty wars between clans over the years. However, even those who were once adversaries seemed to have put any animosities aside, at least for the time being, and were now on friendly terms with one another.

In addition to the Douglas, Lindsay and Ogilvy clans, there were clans Dalhousie and Ramsay of Midlothian, Erskine of Renfrewshire, Farquharson, Graham, Guthrie and Hamilton of the lowlands, Logan of East Ayrshire, Lundy of Perthshire, Muirhead and Scrymgeour of Fife, as well as clans Siddald and Stewart.

After a few minutes of allowing the assembled clansmen to renew old acquaintances, Erskine brought the meeting to order by loudly banging a wooden mallet on the table and asking everyone to take their seats.

After an explanation of why this meeting had been called, which was unnecessary since everyone present already knew why they were there, Patrick asked David Lindsay to speak first.

Lindsay gave a rather lengthy explanation of how the Justiciar's position was a hereditary position and if his son was unable to fulfill the requirements of Justiciar, then the position should revert to him since he was the only heir of his son, Alexander, that was of lawful age.

Uncle Alexander then rose and explained how the monks of Arbroath Abbey had appointed him as Justiciar because they were dissatisfied with Alexander Lindsay. He further explained that the monks had been empowered by King James himself to appoint whoever they wished to the position of Justiciar and to also remove anyone from that position if they wished. He then added if this was a hereditary position then neither Lindsay should have been appointed in the first place since the Ogilvys had held the title of

Justiciar through many generations.

After my uncle had finished speaking, Lindsay then asked William Douglas to testify. Douglas rose and strode to the front of the group. He then proceeded to give a long and rambling discourse that seemed to suggest, without actually saying it, that Clan Douglas was the true authority in Angus, if not all of Scotland itself. This didn't sit well with the assemblage and there were many grumblings and sounds of disagreement that were loud enough for Erskine to pound the table with his mallet to restore order.

After Douglas had finished speaking, it was time for the vote. This was accomplished by the clan chieftains or their representatives standing when they were asked who they supported for the Justiciar's position. When asked who supported Lindsay's claim only four men rose, representing the clans of Douglas, Lindsay, Hamilton and Scrymgeour. It was well known that the Hamilton chieftain was heavily in debt to the Douglas clan, and the oldest son of Hugh Scrymgeour was to marry one of the Douglas daughters.

When asked who supported Ogilvy, the remaining eleven representatives all rose. Patrick Erskine abstained from voting. After announcing the vote results, Erskine pronounced Alexander Ogilvy as the true and rightful Justiciar and then banged his mallet once more to disband the meeting.

A number of the men present shook my uncle's hand in congratulations. David Lindsay spoke to no one as he and his attendants quickly left the hall. In order to avoid any confrontation with Lindsay, we waited until we were sure he and his group had left before our group headed for our homes.

The ride home was very pleasant and we were all in high spirits. The question of who was Justiciar had now been decided and my uncle could now get on with the duties that were required of that position. One of the first duties to take care of was making sure Alexander Lindsay was brought to justice. Things that day were looking very bright indeed. It was the next morning that things started going wrong... terribly wrong.

Chapter 20

Early the next morning we were awakened by a terrible pounding on the castle door with someone shouting "Lord Ogilvy!! Lord Ogilvy!"

I was the first one up to see what all the commotion was about. I cautiously unbarred the door and with my sword held tightly in my right hand I allowed the door to swing open slightly so I could peer outside. I was met with a ghastly sight.

A monk from the abbey was standing there in the early morning mist. He had evidently received a wound to the top of his head. Dried blood covered the entire part of the bald spot in front of his tonsure cut. It had also had run down to cover the right side of his face. Even much of the upper part of his robe was black from the dried blood. He was breathing in a rapid breathless manner. The cool dampness of the morning was turning his breath into a white fog that wreathed his face and gave him a ghostly appearance.

"Lord Ogilvy, please, I must speak to the Justiciar right away!" the monk said in a breathless rapid manner. My uncle appeared behind me, still wearing his night clothes. Hearing the monk's request he asked, "I am Alexander Ogilvy. What do you want?"

"The abbey was attacked before dawn this morning by a gang of men. We tried to stop them, but they caught us by surprise and quickly overwhelmed us. At least one of our brothers was killed and a number of us injured," the monk replied.

"Did they rob you?" my uncle asked.

"No, the only thing they were interested in was freeing Alexander Lindsay. Once they had him they quickly left."

"How many men were there?"

"About 10, maybe a few more."

"I'm not entirely surprised to hear this," my uncle said in a low voice, almost to himself. Then addressing the monk he said, "Please, come inside. You're in need of medical attention, some food and rest."

The monk, whose name was Brother Androw, quickly accepted my uncle's invitation. The rest of the castle was now awake. Some of the women had Androw lay down by the fire and set about gently cleaning his wound and washing the dried blood away.

"I should have taken your advice, Campbell, and hung the bastard when I had the chance," my uncle said. "We must get to Arbroath as quickly as we can. Get as many men as you can as quickly as possible; tell them we leave in an hour. Have them travel well-armed."

I did as I was told and in less than an hour I had nearly 20 men together. We were soon on our way to Arbroath, pushing our horses as fast as we could through the early morning mist.

As we came into town the mist had burned away and the sun was well up in the eastern sky. We had ridden hard. The horses were breathing heavily and covered in lather when we finally came to a stop in front of the west gate of the abbey. At least it was where the west gate once stood. Now there was only a gaping hole where a large ram had broken the heavy oaken door apart, the remains of which were lying just inside the doorway.

There was a large crowd in and around the doorway. Some were monks from the abbey but most of them appeared to be townspeople. They were busily occupied in cleaning up the mess from the break in and repairing or replacing the massive doors.

The crowd parted as we rode up and our group entered the abbey and dismounted. There were signs of a violent struggle in the courtyard. In addition to parts of the shattered door, there were broken stools and benches strewn about along with parts of hoes and other farm equipment that the monks had used as weapons. There was even an axe head, covered in blood, which had come off its handle. The bloodied axe head indicating that the monks had at least gotten some blows in against the attackers.

There were a number of monks laying or sitting about the courtyard nursing various injuries. There were also three objects covered with blankets. We found out later they were the mortal remains of two of the abbeys monks that were killed in the fighting along with one of the attackers. One of the monks killed was the elderly man that had assisted at my uncle's swearing in as Justiciar.

My uncle spied Abbot Walter sitting on a bench and being attended to by Morag MacPherson. The abbot's right arm was bandaged and Morag was helping him get his arm into a sling.

The abbot saw us as we walked over to him. "Lord Ogilvy, thank God you've come," the abbot exclaimed. "You're being here must mean Brother Androw made the trip to Inverquharity. How is he doing? I hated to send him with such a bad head wound but he insisted he was ok and I really didn't feel I could spare an able-bodied man. I wasn't sure if those ruffians would return to rob us." The abbot's words came in a torrent, revealing the agitation and stress he was experiencing.

"We came as soon as we heard," my uncle replied. "Brother Androw is being well taken care of. His head wound produced a lot of blood but doesn't appear to be too serious. I'm sure he'll be up and about in no time."

"Well that's good news," the abbot replied. He then continued, "I'm sorry we lost Lindsay, but they took us by surprise. We're not warriors but we did the best we could. They had swords and spears and we had hoes and axes, but we didn't give up. We fought back we did, and we bloodied them some, and…"

"Abbot, you must calm down and rest," Morag suddenly interjected cutting the abbot off. Turning to my uncle she continued,

"Please excuse us, the abbot has been through a lot the past few hours and I need to give him a tonic and get him into bed."

"Abbot Walter, please come with me," Morag said as she gently took him by his uninjured arm and gently guided him toward his quarters. "I'll be back as soon as I get the abbot taken care of," Morag called to us over her shoulder as she walked with him to his lodgings. Evidence of the many severe wounds Morag had been taking care of was in the state of her white hair. The last time I had seen her it was as white as snow but was now stained with blood and grime.

At that moment, a horse and rider coming through the west gate attracted our attention. I was happy to see it was our trainer and now good friend, Sande.

"Hello, Sande, I'm glad to see you," I told him as he stopped his horse in front of us and proceeded to dismount.

"And I'm glad to see you," he replied, "Although I wish the circumstances were a bit better. I heard what happened here from a horse and rider on their way to Aberdeen and came right away. It's a sad day indeed that that scoundrel Lindsay is running loose again." Turning to my uncle, he asked "What action do you plan to take, Lord Ogilvy?"

"Well the first thing we need to do is get the abbey and the monks taken care of. Then we need to bring Alexander Lindsay and his cohorts to justice," My uncle replied. "The question is what is the best way to go about that. My concern is that this was not just a group of Lindsay's friends behind this. It was too well-planned and coordinated. I'm afraid that we might be dealing with the entire clans of Douglas and Lindsay. If that's so, we're going to have a fight on our hands."

"If you wish, Laird Ogilvy, I can ride to Stirling castle and inform King James and his regent of the situation and ask for their assistance," Sande replied.

"I wonder how much good that would do," my uncle replied. "Our good king is related to some of the Douglas's is he not?"

"Aye, William Douglas is actually his cousin but I understand they're not close at all. In fact, I've heard they hate each other. Most importantly, the King's regent, Sir Alexander Livingston of Callendar is no fan of the Douglases. Since James is still a boy, Sir Livingston will be the one making any decisions in this regard," Sande replied.

"In that case, perhaps an appeal to the king and his regent might be helpful. Whatever we do I'm afraid that time is of the essence. How soon do you think you can leave for Stirling Castle?"

"I can leave now," Sande answered.

"Thank you, Sande, that would be splendid. Please take Campbell with you. He'll be good company for the trip and will also be an asset in case you run into Lindsay or any of his followers on your journey." Turning to me Uncle Alexander asked, "Do you mind going with Sande on this mission?"

"I don't mind at all, Uncle," I responded. In truth, I was very happy to go with Sande on this trip. It would be a bit of an adventure and a chance to spend time with my friend. I also felt the need to do something. Even if all we accomplished was having a long ride, that was better than waiting around doing nothing, waiting for Lindsay to act.

"Very good," My uncle said. "Please tell me right away what the king and his regent says. In the meantime, I'll contact some members of the council to see what advice they can offer."

"We should be back at Inverquharity in three days' time, hopefully with good news from the King," Sande replied. With that Sande and I set out on our trip to Stirling Castle.

Chapter 21

Stirling Castle lay a good two-days ride from Arbroath. We covered as much distance that first day as we could. It was after dark by the time we decided to stop for the night. There were no inns around but we knocked on a farmer's door to ask his permission to spend the night in his barn. The farmer was quite unfriendly at first, but Sande gave him a silver coin and it changed his whole demeanor. He not only allowed us to stay in his barn but he also gave us an ample supply of mutton and rye bread for a meal. We thanked the farmer and retired to the barn for the evening. We unsaddled our horses and put them in a fenced area to graze and rest. We then ate the food the farmer had given us and quickly bedded down in a pile of thick straw for the night.

I was woken up shortly before daybreak by a goat that was licking and nuzzling my hair. I wasn't sure what the goat was up to but quickly found out. The goat suddenly chomped down on a sizable clump of my hair and pulled a good deal out with a quick snap of his head. Yelping in pain, I slapped the goat away and jumped up. Sande was already awake and saw what the goat did. He was laughing loudly at my discomfort.

"That's good, Campbell. You're feeding the livestock and getting your haircut at the same time."

I gave Sande the most unpleasant look I could muster, which only made him laugh more. I then stumbled outside still half asleep to find my horse. Sande followed behind me, still laughing.

We quickly got our horses saddled up and were back on the road as the sun was just beginning to show over the distant horizon. We still had some of the mutton left over from the night before that we ate for our breakfast as we rode along, our cloaks wrapped tightly around us to ward off the early morning chill.

The day was uneventful, although a bit cooler and cloudier than it had been the day before. There were a number of light rain showers that we passed through, but thankfully none that soaked through our cloaks. We arrived at a small church just outside of the town of Stirling shortly before sunset. We were not far from the castle, but it was too late to call on the king. We decided to spend the night at the church, if possible, and go to the castle first thing in the morning.

Sande approached a monk that we saw on the grounds and asked his permission to spend the night. The monk was happy to accommodate us and led us to a small building behind the church. The monks name was Brother Johne and he was the caretaker of the church and its outbuildings. He lived alone on the grounds and seemed quite happy for our company. He found us a couple of cots to sleep on and even shared his evening meal of thick stew and bread. After eating our fill, we went straight to our beds, grateful to have cots to sleep on instead of the barn floor of the previous night.

We awoke early the next morning and shook out our kilts and cleaned up our shirts and cloaks the best we could. We shared a breakfast of porridge with the monk. After thanking him and paying him a couple of silver coins, we set out for the castle.

We soon found ourselves at the long ramp that led to the huge imposing structure that was Stirling Castle. After we had gone a short ways up the ramp, a guard came out to meet us and asked us our business. Sande told him briefly that we wanted an audience with the king as soon as possible and that it was a matter of the utmost importance. The fact that Sande was very well dressed and carried the weaponry of a warrior seemed to impress the guard. At any rate the guard didn't question us but simply nodded his head in acknowledgment and asked us to wait while he delivered the message.

I have to admit I was quite nervous about the possibility of meeting the King of Scotland, but Sande seemed to be very nonchalant and relaxed.

In a very few minutes, the guard returned saying, "Please follow me." He then turned and led the way into the castle. We entered through a beautiful and impressive frontispiece that was five stories high. Passing through the frontispiece, we entered the gatehouse that contained three gates, each of which was provided with a portcullis. The top of the gate house was capped with wall walks and conical roofs.

After passing through the gatehouse, we walked through a huge building. After exiting that building we then crossed a bridge and entered the palace itself. We walked a short distance until we came to a large oaken door with numerous carvings of animals and birds. The guard knocked three times loudly on the door and it slowly opened. There were two more guards inside the room and they beckoned us in with a slight bow and a wave of their hands. Upon entering this room, both Sande and I were impressed at how ornate and beautiful it was. There was a large fireplace to our right that was covered with carvings of lions, thistles and eagles. Above the fireplace was hung a huge tapestry of a unicorn. The walls were covered with even larger tapestries depicting hunting scenes and battles. The ceiling of this room was especially impressive as it was covered with beautiful paintings of past kings and other influential people and "worthies."

"Please make yourselves comfortable," one of the guards said. "I will inform the King that you wish to speak with him." He then bowed and left the room. The other guard stayed with us, standing in front of the door the other guard had left from. Both Sande and I took seats in two chairs covered in red leather that were in front of the fireplace.

After taking our seats, Sande leaned over and whispered to me, "Whatever you do, don't stare at the King or show any surprise at the markings on the King's face, He's very sensitive about that."

"What markings?" I inquired.

"The king has a large red mark on his face that he's had since birth. In fact he's acquired the nickname of 'Fiery Face,' not that anyone calls him that to his face," Sande answered.

In less than 30 minutes, the guard had returned and told us, "The King and Sir Livingston will see you now. Follow me please."

We did as instructed and followed the guard into another room as beautiful and ornate as the one we had just left. As we walked into the room, the guard stopped and came to attention. He then intoned in a solemn voice, "Your Highness, I present Alexander Seton and Campbell Ogilvy."

Sitting at a table at the far side of the room was an older gentleman that I assumed was Sir Livingston. To the left of the man sitting at the table, standing looking out a window was a youth of about 14. As we entered the room, the youth turned towards us and the first thing I noticed was there was a large vermillion mark that nearly covered the entire right side of his face.

The surprise of seeing such an unusual mark caused me to completely forget the warning from Sande. I stood there staring at the King's face for a few seconds until a sharp elbow in the ribs from Sande caused me to come to my senses and join him in making a low bow to the King and then a lesser bow to Sir Livingston.

"Welcome to Stirling Castle, gentlemen," Livingston said as he rose from his chair. Turning towards the king, he continued "Allow me to introduce his Highness the Duke of Rothesay and King James II of Scotland."

Sande and I bowed again and the king nodded his head slightly in return.

"Our visitors have a matter of grave importance they wish to discuss. Would your highness care to join us in the discussion?" Livingston asked.

Ignoring the question, James instead walked purposefully towards me, his dark eyes focused intently on mine. He stopped a foot or two in front of me and with his eyes still locked on mine said, "You were staring at me when you first came in. What were you staring at?"

Taken aback by the question, I fumbled for an answer until finally Sande spoke for me, "Your majesty, my friend was just awed to be in your presence."

"Is that right Mr. Ogilvy? You were staring at me because you were awed to be in my presence?" the King asked in a monotone voice, betraying no sign of emotion.

I have to admit I was quite intimidated by the young king. So intimidated in fact I couldn't lie. Finding my voice I finally stammered, "No, Sire, I couldn't help but to notice the mark on your face and I was staring at that. I'm sorry, it won't happen again."

"Thank you for your honesty," the King replied. "Having people lie to you all the time gets so tiresome and I know you won't do that again because if you do, I'll have you hung."

"I understand," I mumbled.

"Now, this grave matter you wish to discuss, I understand it has to do with my relatives the Douglases and their friends the Lindsays, is that correct?" the King continued.

"Yes, Sire, that is correct," Sande answered.

"Well my opinion in this matter carries little weight since I haven't reached the age of majority yet, but I'm sure my regent Sir Livingston will be more than happy to assist you in any disagreement you might have with the Douglases. He hates the Douglases, in fact he's already murdered two of my cousins, haven't you Livingston?"

"Anything I did, Sire, was only to protect you," Livingston responded.

"Anything you do is only to protect and enrich yourself Livingston," the king retorted. "We both know you'd have me thrown in prison as you did my mother if you could get away with it. In fact, you'd probably have me killed if you could figure a way to do it without being held responsible. I really don't care what action you take against the Douglases but please don't try and tell me it's for my benefit. Now if you gentlemen will excuse me I have other matters to attend to," the King said as he turned to leave.

"Sire," Sande began, "please understand we mean no harm to the Douglases. Our problem is really only with Alexander Lindsay, the Master of Crawford."

"Well that's a pity. I do wish harm to come to the Douglases. Even though they are related to me in some way, I've never trusted them. In fact, dislike of the Douglas clan is one of the few things

Livingston and I see eye to eye on," the king replied to Sande before again turning and leaving the room.

"Our King James is quite an outspoken young man," Livingston said before gesturing to us to sit down. "Please tell me how the King may assist you," He continued after we had sat down at the table facing him.

Sande and I then proceeded to relate the details of what had transpired the past several months. We told him of Lindsay's crimes, which included the murders of my father and Laird George and the assault on the abbey. I did most of the talking, but Sande added a few pertinent details. I think Sir Livingston already knew most of what we told him, but he listened intently to all we had to say, nodding his head from time to time.

When we had finished, I asked Sir Livingston, "Can the crown be of any assistance in apprehending Lindsay and his followers, and more importantly, can the crown prevent clans Douglas and Lindsay from impeding my uncle's attempt to bring Lindsay to Justice?"

Sir Livingston remained silent for a moment before responding to my question, "The apprehension of Lindsay and his followers will probably be best left up to your uncle. However, I will have a decree issued over the signature of the king that states that this Alexander Lindsay, otherwise known as the Master of Crawford, is wanted for murder and other crimes. The decree will further state that anyone who aids or assists Alexander Lindsay will be guilty of the same crimes as he is."

"That would be most appreciated," Sande replied.

"You're very welcome," Livingston said. "However, I don't have to tell you that we live in lawless and turbulent times and the Douglases are a very powerful clan. I hope the proclamation will keep Lindsay from receiving any aid but don't be surprised if the clans Douglas and Lindsay ignore it. If they do ignore it and continue providing aid to the Master of Crawford, there is not much the king can do about it at the present time, and unfortunately the Earl of Douglas knows this."

This acknowledgement that clan Douglas was powerful enough to challenge the king himself was unsettling but there was nothing we could do about that. We knew that the proclamation was the best that we could hope for. We thanked Sir Livingston for his help and started on our journey back to Inverquharity.

Chapter 22

It was nearly noon by the time we started back. We rode at a good clip until it was almost dark and then stopped for the night at an inn Sande knew about. He said it was a safe place to spend the night and that they served good food and even better ale. We arrived just before they were serving the evening meal. After bedding the horses in the barn, we found ourselves seats at a long table the innkeeper had set up near the fire. The inn wasn't crowded that night, there being only five other travelers at the table.

A young woman of about 16, whom I assumed was the innkeeper's daughter, brought us tankards of ale. Then the innkeeper himself came around with the evening meal. Sande was right; the food was good as was the ale. We quickly ate and drank our fill. After we finished, the innkeeper came around and collected enough coins from everyone to pay for the meal and the night's lodging. The serving girl brought us more ale and Sande and I lingered at the table awhile, discussing the day's events and letting our food settle.

"What was the King talking about when he said something about Sir Livingston imprisoning his mother and murdering his cousins?" I asked Sande.

"It's all true," he replied. "After King James' father was assassinated, his widow, Queen Joan, married Sir John Stewart. Queen Joan and her new husband, along with the boy king, went to Stirling Castle where Livingston was the warden. Taking advantage of his position as warden he had the Queen and her husband imprisoned there until the Queen made a formal agreement to put young James in his custody. She was also forced to turn her dowry over to Livingston for the king's maintenance, as well as make a statement that Livingston had acted in the best interests of the young king and for his safety."

"About a year later," Sande continued, "Livingston invited the Sixth Earl of Douglas and his 11-year-old brother, David, to visit the king. The two brothers accepted the invitation and when they arrived they were given a royal welcome, treated to a lovely feast, and then taken to the courtyard of the castle and beheaded."

"Why did Livingston kill them?" I asked.

"It was all about power," Sande replied. "Livingston felt, probably correctly, that the Douglases were scheming against the king and the killings were a warning to them."

"Sir Livingston doesn't appear to be the kind of person that is capable of that kind of ruthless behavior," I said, realizing as soon as I said it how naïve that sounded.

"Power can be a very corrupting influence, it sometimes brings out the very worst of human nature," Sande replied.

"Weren't the Douglases outraged at this? I would have thought they would have demanded justice and retribution for a crime that horrendous."

"I'm sure many of them were outraged. However, Sir Livingston didn't act on his own. He had the full backing of the two murdered boy's great uncle, Sir James Douglas. As the seventh Earl of Douglas and their clan chieftain, Sir James was able to prevent any action being taken against Livingston or anyone else that was connected with the murders."

"Why would anyone want to murder their own family members?" I asked in amazement.

"The same motive Livingston had, power. James Douglas thought the two boys were a threat to him so he had them eliminated. With some people, the need to obtain power and then keep it once you have it can be an all-consuming obsession. Douglas appears to be one of those types of people that everything is secondary to their need for power. The nickname given Douglas, "The Gross," appears to be well earned.

"Sadly, it appears that James Douglas's son, William, has inherited his father's obsession. That would explain why we're having a lot of the problems that we're having now."

"Aye, that it would," replied Sande as he tried to stifle a yawn.

By this time, we had finished our ale. The food and drink, along with the long ride we had had, were making us both sleepy. We made our beds by the fire and promptly fell into a deep sleep.

We awoke at daybreak and after a light breakfast of porridge, saddled our horses and resumed our journey. The November sky was overcast and colder than normal for that time of year. Even with our cloaks wrapped tightly around us we still felt the chill. We pushed the horses a bit faster than normal and the extra heat produced from their exertions helped to keep us a bit warmer.

Shortly after noon, we came to a fork in the road. Sande needed to take the left fork to get home and the right led back to Inverquharity. "I don't think I need to accompany you to Inverquharity," Sande said. "You can inform your uncle of what happened as well as I, and I have business to take care of at home. However, please tell your uncle that I am at his disposal whenever he needs me."

I thanked Sande and we said our goodbyes. Sande headed for his home and I continued on to Inverquharity.

My arrival must have been announced because Uncle Alexander came out to meet me as I rode up to the castle. Before I even dismounted, my uncle was inquiring about our trip and what we had accomplished. I told him about the meeting with the king and his regent. My uncle was pleased to hear about the promise of a proclamation from the king declaring Lindsay a wanted man who was to be given no aid or assistance in escaping from justice.

"And how did you fare, Uncle? Were you able to get any offers of assistance from any of the clan chieftains on the council?" I inquired as I led Malice to the barn where I handed him off to Thom.

"Aye," he replied. "Everyone I spoke to was outraged with what's happened and they all pledged support if we need it. However, I only approached those I knew who aren't allied or obligated to the Douglases or Lindsays."

"Well, that's good news that we have so much support." I said.

"Aye, but I've heard Lindsay is gathering supporters as well. I don't mind telling ye, Campbell, this matter has me worried. I don't think this situation will be settled peaceably."

As my uncle and I were talking, Ellene appeared in the doorway of the barn. I noticed that even under her cloak her belly was beginning to show signs of our baby growing within her. She gave me a beautiful smile as she walked over to embrace me. "Welcome home, my husband," she murmured as we held each other.

"Nice to be home," I replied. I couldn't help but marvel at how far away the problems we were facing seemed when Ellene was in my arms.

I was grateful that my uncle smiled and excused himself so that Ellene and I might have some time alone. After our long embrace, we took a walk through the woods. I told her about our meeting with the king and what we had accomplished. She listened in silence but I could tell she was apprehensive about the whole situation.

We stopped when we came to the place where we had made love for the first time. It looked so different now that winter was starting to make its presence felt. We held each other in silence, neither one of us wanting to speak. We were both enjoying the moment and trying to make it last as long as possible.

"My uncle feels this matter with Lindsay is not going to be settled peacefully and I'm afraid he's right," I finally said, breaking the silence.

"Surely the Douglases and Lindsays will not fight against us knowing we have the King's support, will they?" Ellene asked with an almost plaintive voice.

"The Douglas clan is almost as powerful as the king himself. Some say it's more powerful. Even Sir Livingston, the king's regent, said as much when he told us the Douglases might ignore the king's proclamation," I answered.

There was sadness in Ellene's eyes as she said, "Well, whatever is to come we'll face it together."

"Of course we will." I said as I smiled reassuringly at Ellene. At least I hoped it was a reassuring smile. Then we started back for the castle. The sun was starting to disappear below the horizon and it was getting colder. We both wrapped our cloaks tighter about us as we walked hand in hand. I felt a shiver run up my spine and I knew it wasn't just because of the weather.

Chapter 23

The end of the year was now fast approaching. The Christmas season passed quietly and pleasantly. The continuing troubles with Lindsay, although seldom spoken about, were always in our thoughts. They kept the festive season from being quite as joyous as it would have been normally.

True to his word, Sir Livingston had a proclamation issued by the king. It stated that Alexander Lindsay was an enemy of the crown and a fugitive from justice. It called upon all freemen and indentured servants to apprehend Lindsay and turn him over to the Justiciar of Angus, Alexander Ogilvy.

The proclamation further went on to say that no aid or assistance was to be given to Lindsay by any individual or clan and anyone providing aid or assistance would be committing a crime against the king himself and dealt with accordingly.

The proclamation was posted in every town and village throughout the county of Angus. However, just as Sir Livingston predicated, it was completely ignored by those that supported Alexander Lindsay. In fact, the proclamation seemed to have the opposite effect of what was intended. We began receiving word that Clan Chieftain William Douglas was now openly stating his support for Alexander Lindsay to be Justiciar. He made it clear that it was his intent to reinstate Lindsay as Justiciar, at the point of a sword if necessary.

Lindsay's exact whereabouts were unknown to us but it was obvious that he was still in Angus and still causing trouble. A letter was delivered to Abbot Walter. The letter demanded that the abbot "immediately reinstate the Master of Crawford, Alexander Lindsay, to his rightful position as Justiciar of Angus and that any imposters serving in that position be removed from said office." The abbot ignored the letter, which was unsigned, but other attempts to contact and influence the abbot were now being made. Some of those contacts were now coming with threats of violence, unless Lindsay was reinstated as the Justiciar.

It was shortly after the first of the year when Abbot Walter paid a visit to Inverquharity and told us about the contacts from Lindsay and his supporters. It was late on a Monday afternoon on a bitter cold and blustery day. The abbot, my uncle and I were sitting in the great room in front of a warming fire enjoying sips of my uncle's whisky to further ward off the chill of the day.

"Who was it that delivered the letter?" My uncle asked the abbot after the abbot had finished telling us about the letter and the other contacts.

"The person didn't give their name and I didn't recognize him. However, he was wearing the tartan of Clan Douglas. He just handed me the letter and left," the abbot replied. "Since the letter made no threats and was unsigned, I just ignored it. I thought it was probably just a feeble idea that came to Lindsay in one of his drunken stupors. However, with the repeated contacts that we are now having that include threats, I thought it best to inform you of the situation."

"How were the other contacts made, were they letters as well?" I inquired.

"No," said the abbot. "There were two further contacts after I received the letter. One from another man I didn't recognize but who was also wearing the Douglas tartan. He accosted me as I went to the cobbler's shop just outside the abbey walls. He told me if I wished to avoid bloodshed, some of which may be my own, I should reinstate Lindsay as Justiciar."

The abbot paused to take a sip of his drink before continuing.

"The other contact was not with me personally but was the most forceful. Brother Henry had gone to town for some supplies. Two men he didn't recognize grabbed him and pulled him into the close behind the blacksmith shop. One held a knife to his throat while the other said that if Lindsay were not reinstated as Justiciar they and their supporters would burn the abbey to the ground and kill all the monks."

"Those scoundrels!" my uncle exclaimed. "Were these two men also wearing the Douglas tartan?"

"Brother Henry doesn't remember. I'm afraid he was too shaken up to recall what they were wearing or even what they looked like," the abbot answered.

"Well this is a black day indeed," my uncle said in a solemn voice as he refilled the abbot's glass. "It doesn't appear that there will be any way to settle things peacefully."

"It's looking as though there will be bloodshed," the abbot agreed.

"Has anyone been in contact with David Lindsay about this situation?" I inquired. "Laird Lindsay doesn't seem to be the type to flaunt the law and disobey the king in this manner. He knows his son's behavior was so outrageous that he needed to be removed from office. Maybe this is all being pushed by the Douglases as part of their rivalry with the king. It could be David Lindsay isn't even aware that all this is happening."

"I doubt that David isn't aware of what's going on," my uncle replied. "However, I suppose that it wouldn't hurt to make sure. Perhaps Campbell and I could pay David Lindsay a visit and find out if he knows what's going on and what his suggestions are."

"A visit couldn't hurt and it may produce some good," said Abbot Walter. "However, I don't think you and Campbell should go. David Lindsay might think you're trying to make him chose your side against his son for your personal gain. Let me go instead.

Lindsay might think of me as being more impartial than you two. He might be more willing to listen to reason if the arguments come from me rather than you."

"Your suggestion makes sense, Abbot," my uncle said. "What do you think, Campbell?" my uncle asked, turning towards me.

"I think the abbot's right," I agreed. "Any ideas coming from him would carry much more weight than those same ideas coming from us."

"Well, if you're willing to do that, Abbot, it would be much appreciated," said my uncle.

"I would be honored to do that," replied the abbot. "I'll leave for Finavon Castle first thing in the morning."

"Thank you so very much. If I may make a suggestion, since it's late, why don't you have your evening meal with us and spend the night here? Leaving from here will save you a few miles on your trip to Lindsay's castle."

Abbot Walter quickly accepted my uncle's offer, and after a delicious meal prepared by Besse, we turned in early.

The abbot got an early start in the morning, leaving shortly after daybreak. "If all goes well, I should be back this way before nightfall," he called to us as he rode off to see David Lindsay.

True to his word, the abbot returned to Inverquharity in the late afternoon. My uncle and I were alerted to his return by Thom, who spied him when he turned up our lane. We were waiting outside when the abbot rode up.

"I have good news," the abbot began as soon as his horse slowed to a stop and he began dismounting. "The Earl was very glad to see me. He professed no knowledge of what his son has been up to and appeared sincerely upset at what has taken place. He pledged to do all he can to defuse this situation."

"That is wonderful news!" my uncle exclaimed. "Perhaps this unfortunate matter can be settled without bloodshed after all."

"Aye, perhaps it can," the abbot agreed. "I don't think David Lindsay would assist us in apprehending his son but I sincerely think he will do anything in his power to keep his son from regaining the position of Justiciar through the use of violence. He made a point of saying that he would forbid any of his clansmen from supporting anyone who wished to settle the manner with the sword."

"Thank you for what you've done, Abbot," my uncle said as he instructed Thom to take the abbot's horse. "I insist you spend the night with us. It's much too late to travel back to the abbey tonight."

The abbot, who looked very tired and a bit bedraggled from his travels, smiled slightly saying, "Well, I guess I could be persuaded to stay the night. I don't think there's anything at the abbey that can't wait until I get back."

"Splendid!" my uncle said as he led the way back into the castle where we enjoyed another sumptuous meal provided by Besse. A meal that was interrupted by many toasts to the abbot, to David Lindsay, and to the prospect of long term peace for the citizens of Angus.

I remember that evening as one of great relief and happiness. I think everyone felt as if a great weight had been lifted from our shoulders and that the prospect of a peaceful solution was at hand.

That good feeling was still prevalent as we saw the abbot off in the morning. In fact that good feeling lasted nearly three days, until the Sabbath, January 16th. That was the day the ultimatum was received by the abbot.

Chapter 24

The ultimatum was nailed to the west door of the abbey, just below the abbot's quarters. No one saw who delivered it. It was discovered in the early afternoon after services. It was such an outrageous document that it would have been humorous if it had not contained the certain threat of violence and that we knew it had the full backing of the Douglas clan.

The ultimatum read as follows:

"We, the citizens of Angus will no longer tolerate the illegal and unjust appointment of Alexander Ogilvy as Justiciar. We demand the immediate reinstatement of the rightful holder of that position, Alexander Lindsay.

"We have tried numerous times to arbitrate this usurpation of the rightful authority in Angus in a peaceful manner without success. We now have no choice but go the route of arbitrament by the sword. That being the recourse that has been forced upon us, one week hence, the citizens of Angus will gather in arms at the west gate of the abbey at Arbroath and see that justice is done and the Master of Crawford, Alexander Lindsay, is restored to his position as Justiciar of Angus."

Copies of this ultimatum were made and delivered to a number of towns and villages throughout Angus. It made no difference to the authors of the document that the citizens of Angus, excepting the Douglases and Lindsays, were against Lindsay being reinstated. It also made no difference that the rightful authority in Angus was King James acting through his appointee, Abbot Walter. The Douglases were exerting their claim to power and were willing to use violence to get it, even defying the King himself.

"An outrage! They're defying all legal authority, even the king!" my uncle exclaimed. We were in the abbot's quarters at the abbey. At dawn, the day after the ultimatum had been received, a monk from the abbey had arrived at Inverquharity. In a breathless and excited voice, the monk told us of the demand and threat. I immediately sent word to Duncan and Malcome, and they, along with Uncle Alexander and I, had ridden into Arbroath that afternoon.

"What do you suggest we do?" the abbot asked in a calm voice that hid the apprehension that he must have been feeling.

"Well one thing we won't do is allow these scoundrels to get away with this," my uncle replied. "If they wish to have a fight, then I'll see to it that they get more than they bargained for." In a calmer voice he continued, "We should make sure David Lindsay is aware of this."

"I've already seen to that," The abbot replied. "I sent one of my monks, Brother Enos, to notify David Lindsay the same time I sent Brother James to notify you. I also sent another monk to notify the king."

"Very good," responded my uncle. Turning to the rest of us, he continued, "Campbell, you, Malcome and Duncan spread the word throughout Angus. Make sure all the clans know what is happening and ask for their support. Ask them to join us at Inverquharity by next Friday. Tell them to bring their weapons and as many men as they can."

The three of us nodded our heads in agreement and set off to do as my uncle instructed. It was decided among us that Duncan would take the northern part of Angus. He would go to Auchmithie first, then to Montrose, over to Brechin and then down through Aberlemno stopping to see as many of the Lairds and Freemen as possible. Malcome agreed to head south, through Carnoustie, Monifieth and then on to Dundee and then back through Liff & Benvie. I was to head west, through Letham, Friockheim and Forfar, going as far as Clova and then head back through Dylerhead and Balinbore.

None of us were looking forward to our trip. It would take us all at least two days to complete and it would be dangerous if we ran into any of Lindsay's supporters along the way.

"Tak' caur ye twa. Ee weel see ye in a coople ay days. Watch oot fur Lindsay an' his cronies," Duncan called to us as he climbed into his saddle.

"And you take care as well Duncan, and you also Malcome," I answered.

"Make sure ye twa nae bide it ay th' pubs an' stay awa' frae th' wenches", Malcome said with a smile on his face as he waved us off.

The two days I was traveling were very cold. One of the days I was caught in a sudden storm that started out as snow but then changed to rain, soaking me and chilling me to the bone. However, as bad as the weather was, the reception I received from the lairds and freemen I called on more than made up for any discomforts. The strong assurances of support warmed me emotionally and the frequent offers of food, and drams of whisky that I gratefully accepted, warmed me physically. As my trip progressed, I was in good spirits and began feeling more and more optimistic about the whole situation.

Most of those that I called on were already aware of the ultimatum and pending confrontation, and almost everyone was supportive of my uncle. The vast majority promised to be at Inverquharity no later than Friday. Many of the larger landowners also said they would bring others with them.

I had no run-ins with any of the Douglas or Lindsay supporters, but I did make a point of giving a wide berth to any farms or settlements that I knew were aligned with either of those clans.

I spent Monday night with a distant relative in a tower castle just outside of Clova. The occupant of the castle, Laird George Findlater, was a wealthy landowner with a lot of resources at his disposal. His mother had been an Ogilvy. He very quickly and generously agreed to support us against Lindsay. He promised to be at Inverquharity with no less than 10 men that were all experienced fighters and that would be well equipped.

By late Tuesday I had completed my rounds and was back at Inverquharity. I was happy that Ellene was waiting for me as I entered the castle. The warmth of the fire coupled with the warmth of Ellene's embrace could not have been a more perfect ending to my trip. Although I was still apprehensive about what Sunday would bring I was buoyed by the assurances of support I had received. I felt confident we would prevail.

I quickly related to my uncle all that had happened. He was tremendously relieved to hear my good news. He informed me that Malcome, who had returned about an hour before I did, had met with similar support.

Duncan didn't return until late the next morning, but he was also happy to report that his trip had been as successful as ours. The mood at Inverquharity, which had been somewhat somber, was now relaxed and almost jovial. It was as if a great weight had been lifted from our shoulders.

The afternoon of the same day Duncan returned saw the first of the men we had recruited arriving at Inverquharity. That was on Wednesday, and it was only a few men but by Thursday large numbers began arriving. On Friday, Inverquharity seemed like it was going to be overrun with a flood of armed warriors.

Some arrived on horseback, some on foot and some in wagons. Some were full men at arms with armor, mail, swords and shields. Others were just farmers, armed with axes and hoes and maybe an occasional rusty sword.

On Friday the men from Clova, led by George Findlater, arrived. There were ten men in their group and they were an impressive sight. All had full suits of armor that had been polished until they shown brightly, even in the dull sunshine of that January day. They were all mounted on fine steeds and they even had a wagon with them containing additional weapons and supplies.

The majority of the men were from Angus and were Ogilvies and the Septs of Clan Ogilvy, with surnames such as Airlie, Findlater, Gilchrest, MacGilghrist, Mine, Richardson and Storey. We also had the support of a great many other clans. Some of those clans were from well outside Angus, such as Forbes of Pitslgo, Gordon of Barrowfield, Oliphant of Aberdagie, Maxwell of Tealing and Brucklay of Gartley.

We accommodated as many people as possible inside the castle walls, but it was impossible to accommodate them all. The fields around Inverquharity were now filled with tents and the woods around Inverquharity rang with the sound of axes harvesting wood for their campfires. At night there were so many fires it made me think of fireflies on a summer evening.

Uncle Alexander opened up our storehouses to feed the army. Even that was not enough to feed everyone, so we had to buy many provisions from nearby farms as well as harvest some of the wild game that abounded in the surrounding woods.

Friday evening was quiet. Most everyone had their evening meal shortly after dark and were preparing to turn in early, so as to be well rested for our trip to Arbroath in the morning.

Duncan and Malcome had taken their meal with those of us in the castle. It was crowded and hot with all the extra people. After we had eaten, the three of us walked outside for a breath of air. We stood for a few seconds watching the campfires. No one said anything but I'm sure we all shared the same thoughts.

"Weel, thes time twa nichts hence everythin' will be decided," Malcome said, finally breaking the silence.

Duncan and I murmured our agreement and, without any further conversation, all three of us returned to the castle and to our beds. I was the last one to go back in and I took one last look at the campfires that were now beginning to die down. I couldn't help but wonder how many men sleeping near those fires tonight would still be alive Sunday evening.

Chapter 25

Saturday morning dawned overcast with a slight rain that was more of a mist. The gray, cloudy sky held the possibility of more precipitation. The cold chill in the air indicated that it might come in the form of snow.

When I awoke, it was still dark. Ellene was also awake, and we hugged and held each other. We made love that morning and afterwards held each other tight for a long while before I got out of bed.

By the time I had dressed and assembled my weapons, the castle was fully awake. I kissed Ellene goodbye and held her tight once more before leaving our bedchamber. "Stay safe, Campbell," Ellene murmured with a tear in her eye. "I will," I replied as I left the room and headed down the stairs.

There was a large vat of porridge simmering over the fire in the kitchen. I helped myself to a large serving of it before looking for a seat in the great hall. I found space next to Malcome and Duncan at one of the long tables and benches we had set up to handle the large numbers taking meals at the castle.

Although the hall was completely full I was surprised at how quiet it was. There were a few people engaged in conversation, but most of those assembled seemed alone with their own thoughts. The three of us also sat quietly as we ate our porridge. I forced myself to finish everything on my plate even though food was the last thing I wanted at that moment.

After breakfast, the three of us went outside. There were still clouds in the sky. The rain had stopped and the sun, now well above the horizon, was beginning to burn through the clouds.

The area around Inverquharity was a beehive of activity. Tents were being struck and horses saddled. Men that had them were strapping on their weapons and armor. Father Maclaren had come from Kirremuir along with some monks to assist him. They were moving among the men, giving communion, and stopping to pray with them. The three of us stopped to take communion from one of the monks and receive his blessing. We then joined the large group of men that were starting to form at the front of the castle.

My uncle had appointed Sande's father, Alexander Seton-Gordon, to head up our force. He was a good choice since he had the most military experience of anyone there and was well liked and respected. Sir Gordon was getting our men divided into three groups. As I was walking towards the closest group, he walked up to me saying, "Ah, Campbell, just the man I wanted to speak with. May I have a moment of your time?"

"Of course," I replied.

"As you can see, I'm dividing our force into three groups," the Earl began. "I'm going to have us positioned at the west gate of the abbey. One group, the largest, will be in the center and the other two groups will be on either side to protect our flanks. George Findlater of Clova will be in charge of the center group. I've asked Sande to be in charge of the group on the left and he has agreed to do that. Sande has informed me that you've become skilled with the weapons of war and show a lot of leadership. I would like you to be in charge of the men covering our right flank. Will you agree to take charge of that group?"

I was happy that Sande and his father were on speaking terms and getting along well enough that Sande's father had asked him to be in charge of part of our force. I was also flattered that the Earl thought that I had the ability to lead a group of men in battle. I only wished I had that much confidence in myself. Even though I was made quite nervous by the prospect of taking on so much responsibility I quickly agreed to his request. I replied to the Earl, "I'd be happy to, Sir Gordon, and I'm honored that you asked me. I just hope that I do the job that's expected of me."

"Splendid," the Earl said smiling. "I'm quite confident that you will serve us well. It's getting late. We need to be on the road as soon as possible so that we're prepared to give Lindsay and his friends a proper welcome when they arrive in Arbroath."

"There is one thing sir. Will it be all right if I have my friends Duncan and Malcome in my group?"

"That will be fine. Now please join your men. We need to get them going."

"Thank you," I replied and headed off to join the group of which I had been put in charge. Duncan and Malcome joined me and I quickly told them of my new responsibilities. I could tell they were happy for me, but I had to endure a certain amount of ribbing from them.

"Imagine 'at, uir mukker Campbeel in charge ay darn near ay a whole blledin army. Next hin' we ken he'll be hobnobin' wi' th' king' himself." Duncan said after I had told him and Malcome the news.

"Hobnobin' wi' th' king'?" Malcome responded with mock surprise in his voice. "At th' rate Campbeel is goin, heel be th' king' hiself afair lang."

"You two had better hope I never become king," I told them. "The first thing I'd do is behead you both." I was glad to be engaging in this banter. It was helpful to take our minds off what lay ahead.

The three groups that Gordon had divided us into had a grand total of about 1100 men. The largest group, the one that was to be the center of our line, numbered about 600. The two flanking groups were about 250 men each. About half of each group consisted of vassals and servants who were armed with the most rudimentary of weapons; hoes, shovels, axes and an occasional rusty sword or ancient spear. The other half was more properly attired. A few of them, such as the men from Clova and Sir Gordon's group, were kitted out with all the weaponry and armor of a full man-at-arms.

Sir Gordon began to address the assembly. He had to shout to make himself heard. He first explained the reasoning of our being divided into three groups and then he introduced the leader of each group. When he introduced me, I felt the blood rush to my head and I hoped no one would notice what I feared might be my very red face.

He then went on to tell us of the importance of what we were about to do and the necessity of everyone doing their job. The Earl told how we were sure to be the victors since we were in the right, and God was therefore on our side. I've unfortunately heard similar speeches a number of times since then, but at that time, it was all new, and I have to admit I was inspired by it.

When Gordon had finished, he called Father Maclaren to the front who had us all kneel as he said a prayer for our safety and our victory. When the good Father had finished, Gordon returned to the front, this time with a piper. At a signal from the Earl the piper began to play. Our three groups, led by the Earl and my uncle, began the 23-mile march to Arbroath.

Chapter 26

We arrived at the abbey around mid-afternoon and quickly set up camp. The huge number of men quickly filled the courtyard and other open spaces inside the walls. Many men had to pitch their tents outside the abbey grounds. The abbot offered to share his quarters with my uncle and Earl Gordon but they refused, preferring to pitch their tents with the rest of the men.

After our tents were set up, we started fires to ward off the cold and to cook our evening meal. We had two large wagons filled with food, more than enough for everyone to eat their fill with plenty left over for tomorrow. My uncle had also made arrangements for several casks of good quality ale to be delivered to us.

We soon had a feast prepared. The ample food and limitless amounts of ale gave our gathering an almost festive mood. I was amazed at how jovial everyone seemed. It was as if we were gathered for a celebration instead of a battle, that on the morrow, would undoubtedly claim the lives of many of those gathered.

The ample quantities of food and ale, coupled with the long march we had made, began to take its toll. With the exception of a few guards that the Earl had posted about our camp, we were all soon sleeping soundly in our tents.

After an uneventful night, we began to stir just as the sun was beginning to show above the eastern horizon. I dressed and had a breakfast of porridge along with some leftover mutton. As I was finishing breakfast, a messenger brought me word that Earl Gordon wished to meet with me and the other leaders.

I quickly finished my meal and made my way to where the Earl had pitched his tent. By the time I arrived, Findlater of Clova and Sande were already there as well as my uncle.

"Good morning, gentlemen, I trust you slept well," Gordon said in greeting. "I think everything has been done in preparation for our visit from Lindsay. As soon as our scouts return to let us know that he's on the march, we'll form up into our positions. Does anyone have any questions?"

We had a few minor questions about tactics and formations but we already knew most of what we had to do. We spent a few minutes talking quietly, the festive mood of last night now replaced with a serious and somber mood. Judging from the others conversation I thought they seemed relaxed and confident about the upcoming battle. I hoped I appeared as relaxed and confident as they did. I know I didn't feel that way inside. After our discussion, we returned to our separate groups to await news of Lindsay's force. We didn't have long to wait.

It was shortly after noon that one of our scouts galloped up. Lindsay and his supporters were on the move and they would probably be at the abbey in little more than an hour.

The news that Lindsay and his followers were on the move spread quickly and started a whirlwind of activity. Fires were extinguished, armor or whatever battle dress each man had available was put on and weapons were secured and made ready.

I didn't have a full suit of armor but I did have more protection than most; a coif of mail to protect my head and shoulders, a thick brigandine to cover my chest and abdomen, and greaves and cuisses for my legs. What I had was older and secondhand, but it was of good quality. I had confidence it would give me lots of protection in battle. It was also much lighter and gave me more freedom of movement than a full suit of armor would. After getting into my armor, I strapped on my sword and made sure my axe was secure in the holster attached to my right side.

When we were dressed for battle, we quickly moved the men outside the abbey to get them into proper position in front of the huge oaken doors of the west gate. The men with the most military experience and training along with proper armor were in the front row of our groups and the rest filled in behind. When everyone was properly positioned we had formed a three-sided semi-circle in front of the west gate. Both ends of our formation ended against brick walls to prevent any attacks against our flanks.

Off in the distance a cloud of dust was beginning to appear, proof that Lindsay and his supporters were indeed on their way. It was still a ways off, but the size of the cloud indicated that Lindsay's force was very large, probably larger than our own.

Earl Gordon was still mounted and he rode in front of our assembly. His full suit of polished armor shone brightly. The plume that hung from his helmet was a tartan of Clan Gordon and it matched the caparison of his destrier. On both the plume and the caparison were numerous reproductions of the Gordon coat of arms that was the same as on the shield that the Earl carried. He was an impressive and reassuring sight. He rode back and forth inspecting our formation and then stopped and gave a few words of encouragement. It was much the same speech he had given before our march from Inverquharity, but I was still impressed and awed by it.

After the Earl had finished speaking, Abbot Walter addressed our group. He had us all kneel as he led us in a prayer asking for Divine intervention to protect our forces and to grant us victory over our enemy. The abbot then said a few words in Latin that I don't think anyone understood. When he finished speaking, he made the sign of the cross and walked back toward the abbey.

Now there was nothing left for us to do but wait. Soon the first of Lindsay's force came into town. Leading the way was Alexander Lindsay himself accompanied by William Douglas. They were both outfitted in full suits of armor that had been polished to a bright finish that shown brightly.

Lindsay led his force to a point directly opposite us and about 100 yards away. They looked to number about 2000 men and their ratio of fully armed and equipped men to those armed with farm implements was similar to ours. They quickly formed up in a rectangle with their best armed and equipped men in their front row and the others lined up behind them.

When Lindsay had his men lined up as he wanted them, he and Douglas, along with a third man I didn't recognize, rode their horses into the area between the two opposing forces. They stopped about halfway between the two and Lindsay called out to my uncle, "Laird Ogilvy, I would have a word with you."

My uncle glanced at Gordon who indicated they should meet with Lindsay. My uncle then looked at me and with a nod of his head indicated he wanted me to join them. The three of us rode out to meet with Lindsay and the two others.

As our trio pulled up near Lindsay, he smiled and addressed Uncle Alexander in a friendly manner. "I think you know William Douglas but allow me to introduce Lord James Hamilton, clan chieftain of Clan Hamilton from Clydesdale."

"A pleasure to meet you," my uncle replied as he nodded to Lord Hamilton. "This is Sir Alexander Seton-Gordon of Gordon, the Earl of Huntly, and this is my nephew, Campbell Ogilvy."

Lindsay acknowledged the introductions with a slight bow of his head before continuing in an almost apologetic tone of voice, "This matter has gotten entirely out of hand. There is no need for bloodshed. Simply surrender to me and confess to the crime of illegally rebelling against the lawfully appointed Justiciar of Angus. If you do that, I promise you a quick death and I also promise that there will be no repercussions against any of your supporters and your family will be allowed to keep all your land."

"That's very generous of you," my uncle replied "However, if anyone is to be given death, quick or otherwise, it will be a scoundrel like you. Unfortunately, if I do have to have you put to death I can't guarantee that your family will be able to keep any of your lands. Your crimes have been so monstrous and costly your lands will be forfeited to compensate your victims."

Lindsay's face flushed, at least the part that wasn't covered by his beard and he roared back, "You're a stupid son of a toad and I'll have the satisfaction of putting my sword through your heart before this day is over."

"Tsk, such a pity," Uncle Alexander responded sarcastically. "We were getting along so well too. I guess it's understandable though that someone like you is so quick to anger. It must be terribly stressful not having the faintest idea who your father could be."

"You bloody bastard!" Lindsay screamed as he went for his sword.

"Control yourself!" Douglas shouted as he grabbed Lindsay's arm to keep him from drawing his weapon.

Lindsay glared at my uncle and looked like he was going to say something else but instead wheeled his horse about and galloped back to his lines.

"It's a shame Lindsay had to leave so suddenly," my uncle said. "I was truly beginning to enjoy our conversation."

The three of us shared a laugh as we watched Lindsay and his friends depart and then we too turned our horses and returned to our lines. I have to admit I quite enjoyed the confrontation with Lindsay. I was amused and surprised at how easily Lindsay was to anger, to the point of losing control.

Both of our forces now stood facing each other, neither group wanting to be the first to make a move. It was at this moment a lone rider was seen galloping at a fast pace towards us. At the time I didn't know who the rider was but the rider turned out to be David Lindsay and the first tragedy of the day was about to unfold.

Unknown to anyone on our side, David Lindsay had been working feverishly behind the scenes to prevent such an occurrence as he was now galloping towards. We found out later that ever since he had been informed of his son's intentions he had sought help in defusing the situation. He had ridden far and wide calling on different clan chieftains and even had an audience with the king and his regent. Unfortunately, his attempts to find a powerful ally that would help to prevent the violence that was now close to exploding had come to naught.

Knowing that he might not be able to get to Arbroath before the deadline his son had given as the time he would take back the Justiciar's position by force, Lindsay had sent a messenger in his place. The messenger carried a proclamation from Lindsay that he as clan chieftain was forbidding any member of clan Lindsay from taking part in any armed struggle to restore his son to the position of Justiciar. Once his message had been delivered, the messenger was to return to Lindsay with a report of how the message was received.

Unfortunately that messenger had been ambushed on the road, knocked senseless and left tied up in the ruins of an abandoned farmhouse. It was not until after the battle was over that the messenger managed to free himself.

With his attempts to find an ally to help prevent violence unsuccessful and with no word from his messenger, David Lindsay was now riding towards us in a last desperate attempt to deliver his message himself. According to witnesses that saw him when he first appeared, Lindsay had tied a length of white linen to the top of his sword. As he rode towards us, he carried the sword high above his head so everyone could see the white linen which declared his peaceful intent.

Unfortunately, by the time Lindsay was close enough for us to see him clearly, the linen had come off the sword. We knew nothing of the peaceful and honorable intentions of the horseman riding toward us. All we saw was someone galloping towards us at a high rate of speed with a sword raised high above his head. We thought this was the start of the attack.

There is no way of knowing what effect Lindsay's order to the members of his clan would have had because Lindsay never got a chance to deliver that message. As he rode his horse between the two groups of armed men he slowed his pace a bit but he was still coming our way with his sword held high above his head.

"Ah beleife 'at fellaw has come within mah range." Duncan said as he hefted his spear and made ready to throw.

I had a premonition that maybe we shouldn't try to skewer the fellow on the horse. However, like everyone else I thought the attack was beginning so I made no attempt to stop Duncan. I also thought that at that range, which was now about 50 yards, he was just going to waste a spear. I underestimated Duncan's ability.

Duncan reared back and with all his might gave a mighty grunt as he threw the spear at the figure on the horse. I remember that scene vividly: the long black spear beginning a high arc towards the horse and rider, the horse covered in a white lather from its exertions on the long ride, and the rider sitting motionless in the saddle as the spear hurtled towards him.

What had seemed like an impossible shot was now looking less so as the spear continued on its journey coming relentlessly closer to its target. The rider still sat motionless as if he was transfixed by the deadly object. I still wonder sometimes why David Lindsay made no attempt to get away from the trajectory of the spear. Maybe he didn't know which way to go or maybe he didn't want to show fear or maybe he just assumed he was safe at the distance he was from us. At any rate, Lindsay sat on his horse and continued staring at the object hurtling towards him. At the last second, he did jump back slightly in the saddle and swung his sword at the spear, but it was too late to stop the missile coming at him.

The point of the spear struck Lindsay on the left side of his face.

It went completely through his mouth and exited through the back of his neck, severing his spinal cord as it did so. Lindsay dropped his sword as he was flung backwards off his horse. The horse reared upward, its eyes wide with fear, and nearly toppled over as Lindsay fell to the ground. David Lindsay was dead long before he hit the ground and any chance of a peaceful settlement that day died with him.

The sight of his father dying such a violent death didn't deter his son from engaging in a bit of treachery. Alexander Lindsay, who with his father's death, was now the new Earl of Crawford, walked out in front of his men and shouted a challenge to us.

"Why do you fight with goads as if you were dealing with oxen? Pray, throw them away and let us fight this out with our swords, hand to hand, by true valor, as becomes men!"[1]

We unfortunately accepted this challenge and threw our spears away as it appeared the men on Lindsay's side were doing. However about 100 of the men from Clydesdale kept their spears. As Lindsay's force came towards us these Clydesdale men held their spears by the tops and trailed them at their backs.

Lindsay's force now came at us in a rush as we formed a stout shield wall. All the men in front locked their shields with the men standing next to them as we prepared for the attack. I think our shield wall was strong enough and had enough experienced fighting men that we could have repulsed this attack if we had kept our spears. However, as the two forces closed and the sound of swords

---

[1] *"History of Arbroath"* by George Hay. 2nd Edition 1899

striking shields rang out along with the sounds of men swearing and grunting as the shield walls closed, the Clydesdale men rushed forward with their spears. They thrust their points over the shields of our men and into their chests and faces.

There were no finer or braver men than the ones that fought with us that day, but no man can stand up to spear points being thrust in their face when they don't have a similar weapon with which to defend themselves. The total surprise at seeing weapons that we had not expected caused total confusion which led to panic among our men and our shield wall quickly broke.

Lindsay's forces quickly moved to the slaughter and their swords were finding their mark as our forces tried to regroup. Although I had seen plenty of blood and violence when Arbroath had been attacked by Lindsay and his cohorts it was nothing on the scale that I was witnessing now.

I was saddened to see that one of the first of our men to be struck down was George Findlater of Clova. Cut off and surrounded when our shield wall broke, George went down bravely. He continued to thrust and slash with his sword even as many spear points and sword thrusts were finding their way though chinks in his armor.

The ground all in front of the west gate was being stained red with the blood being spilt from limbs and heads that were being cut off and torsos that were being sliced open.

One of our men standing a few paces in front of me had lost his shield and when a sword blow came at him he raised his left hand to ward it off and he caught the blade between his thumb and index finger. The blade neatly sliced off his thumb and kept going to slice deeply into his shoulder, nearly severing his arm which dropped limply at his side. It didn't keep him from fighting back though. He swung his own sword with his right arm, catching his assailant in the face who then dropped his weapon in order to grab at his wound which was flowing blood.

My group of men fared much better than the ones who were in the center group. The ones who were in the center suffered the full force of the attack and it was their shield wall that broke under the surprise assault of the men with spears.

When I saw the center shield wall giving way, I quickly ordered my men to change directions and we formed a new shield wall with one end of the wall against a corner of the abbey and the other end against a brick structure on the other side of the road that ran past the abbey. Some of our men even had time to retrieve their spears that they had previously thrown down and we were now able to face the enemy from a strong defensive position.

A large number of the men that had been in the center and on the left flank were now able to make a fighting retreat behind our new defense. However, Lindsay's forces wasted no time in continuing their ferocious attack. They were in a killing frenzy, spurred on by their initial success.

They slammed into our shield wall with all the frenzy of mad men, screaming and yelling as they slammed their shields against ours and slashed and stabbed with their swords. They had men with spears rushing forward in an attempt to again break our wall but this time we also had spears with which to hold them at bay.

I was in the shield wall next to Malcome. Duncan was right behind us with a spear that he was using to good effect. Our shields were now pressed tightly against the shields of our enemy. Both sides were pushing and shoving trying to force an opening in the others wall.

We were so close to the enemy that I could smell the foul breath coming from the man in front of me and see his broken yellow stained teeth. He was yelling curses at me and I could feel some of his spittle hitting my face as he continued to yell and scream obscenities.

I had my sword in my hand but I couldn't use it properly due to the confined space we were in. I thought of dropping my sword and pulling my axe when the fellow in front of me made the mistake of letting his foot protrude in front of the shield line as he attempted to gain more leverage. The man was wearing sabatons but they appeared to be cheaply made with thin metal. I quickly stabbed my sword down and had the satisfaction of feeling the blade go completely through his foot as the point embedded itself in the ground. The man howled in pain as he tried to wrench his foot back that was now securely fastened by my sword. It wasn't until his struggles caused the sharp edge of my blade to slice completely through his foot was he able to pull back and move out of the wall.

Although another man quickly took the place of the man I had wounded, the momentary loss of a man in their shield wall enabled our side to move their line back slightly and throw them off balance.

Before they could reform their line, I was able to get enough space to swing my sword at the head of the man to my left. As my sword was arcing down towards his head, the fellow made the mistake of raising his shield to block my sword instead of ducking down. His shield did catch my sword, but when he raised his shield it gave Malcome enough of a target to drive his sword through the lower part of the man's abdomen.

As Malcome pulled his sword out, twisting it slightly as he did so, a great gush of blood along with a good deal of the poor man's intestines came out as well.

A spear point came over the top of my shield but I was able to move my head in time and it missed. Duncan grabbed the spear as it went past my head and pulled it away. As Duncan pulled the spear, the man who had thrust it was thrown off balance and for a brief instant his head and shoulders appeared between the shields. That instant was enough time for Duncan to throw his own spear into the man's neck who then fell to the ground with blood spurting from his wound.

The loss of two more of Lindsay's men caused their shield wall to weaken further. Sensing this weakening, our lads became all the more energized and intensified their effort. Pushing and shoving we could feel Lindsay's wall give ground inch by inch as we continued our ferocious assault. Then, in an instant, their wall buckled and then broke completely. With great howling and cheering our side burst through what had been the Lindsay's shield wall and we were among the enemy. Now it was our turn to commit slaughter.

We tore into the Lindsays with a vengeance. The blood lust was among us all as we began cutting, slashing, and bludgeoning the enemy, all the while yelling and screaming our war cries.

A man to my left raised his shied to block a sword swing from Malcome and as he did so I brought my own sword down hard onto his arm, cutting it off at the elbow. As Malcome finished the man off with a sword thrust through his chest, I swung my sword with a strong backhand motion at another Lindsay that had turned to run. The sharp edge of my sword struck him in the neck and completely severed his head. As his body was falling to the ground, a great spout of red frothy blood shot from his neck.

All around me there was a terrible slaughter. Duncan had regained his favorite weapon and was slashing, stabbing and bludgeoning any Lindsay who was unfortunate enough to get anywhere near him and his spear. The ground was becoming littered with the bodies of our foe.

However, the Lindsays were beginning to regroup. They had formed another shield wall behind which their forces were gathering and I could hear the new Earl of Crawford shouting "Shields together! Shields together!" to his men as their lines stabilized.

We could have probably broken through this shield wall as well since Lindsay's forces were still disorganized and a handful of his men could even be seen running from the battle but a new danger now appeared. Some of our men began shouting "They're coming at us from the rear!" When I turned I could see that a large group of Lindsay's men had indeed circled around behind us and was beginning to form a shield wall to the rear of our forces. The numerical superiority of the Lindsay's enabled them to attack us from two sides. With a growing sense of alarm I realized we were in danger of being trapped between two shield walls.

"Campbell! Campbell!" I heard Gordon shouting my name. "We're in danger of being trapped here; we must break through that shield wall," Gordon said as he pointed towards the new wall forming at our rear. "Take your men and break through that wall and lead them out of town towards the Loan of the Leys. We'll pick a new spot to regroup. I'll keep a group of men with me in the rear to fight off any of Lindsay's forces that pursue us."

I nodded my head vigorously to show Gordon that I understood him and turned to the men gathered about me. "You heard him, let's get through that wall. Duncan, you and all the others that have spears, throw them at the men in the center of the line." With amazing speed, Duncan and five others quickly drew back and loosed their spears as one.

Three of the spears were deflected by the shields without causing injury. However, one spear was thrown under the shields striking a man in the leg and another found its way between the upper portions of two shields and struck a poor unfortunate full in the face. The last spear was thrown by Duncan. It was thrown with such force that although it hit a shield, it went completely through the shield, through the man holding it and even caused injury to a man standing behind him.

The disruption caused by the spears created a weakening in their shield wall as they frantically tried to get replacements for the men that were injured. We took full advantage of that weakness. With great shouts and blood curdling screams we charged that portion of the wall with our shields raised and slammed into the enemy line.

The sound of shields slamming into shields was like a great clap of thunder. We hit them with a force born of desperation and rage. Even if our spears had not disrupted their shield wall I don't think they could have withstood our onslaught. As it was, their line immediately began to give and then quickly broke as we pushed them back and poured through their now broken shield wall.

For the second time that day we had broken through the enemy shield wall, and for the second time that day we could have taken a terrible toll on the enemy. However, even though the group in front of us was in total disarray the rest of Lindsay's force was now attacking us from our rear.

I could hear Gordon yelling for the men he was commanding to close ranks to cover our retreat and I had to resist the urge to attack the disorganized group we had just broken through. With Lindsay's superior numbers we couldn't hope to beat them in the wild melee that the battle was now turning into.

"This way, lads," I yelled at the top of my voice as I led the way from the west gate of the abbey and onto the road to the Loan of the Leys. Our entire force retreated in an orderly fashion, with the men at the very back of our column keeping their swords and shields at the ready in case they needed to form a shield wall to fend off an attack from our rear. Although we had fought well, the tide of battle was favoring the Lindsays and I knew we had to take action to keep our retreat from turning into a slaughter.

Chapter 27

As we made our way toward the Loan of the Leys, I told Duncan to make sure the men kept going and I went back to check on Gordon and our men at the rear. Gordon greeted me with a big smile and clapped me on the back. "Good job, lad," he told me approvingly. Looking at my clothing, he continued, "Looks like you were in the thick of it. Are you injured?"

Glancing down I saw that I was covered in blood; fortunately, none of it was my own. "No injuries, thank God," I replied. "It doesn't appear that Lindsay is continuing the attack," I went on, glancing at the enemy to our rear that didn't appear to be making any movement in our direction.

"Oh, they'll be coming after us," Gordon replied as we walked together. "They're just a bit disorganized right now. There's plenty of daylight left so Lindsay's taking his time getting his troops lined up properly before he has another go at us. We just need to make sure we're ready for when they come at us again."

"Hello, nephew, glad to see you survived the day thus far," a friendly voice behind me said and I turned to see my uncle and James walking towards us. I was quite happy to see they had both survived our initial clash with Lindsay though I noticed James had a wound on the side of his face. There was a white linen bandage that covered his injury that was wrapped from under his chin to the top of his head. A large red splotch on the right side of his face showed where he had been wounded.

"And I'm as glad to see that you both also survived," I responded. "Although I'm sorry to see James has been injured."

"Ah, 'tis but a scratch. One of their spear points in their initial attack grazed my cheek. It will heal quickly," James replied confidently.

"I think we can be proud at how well we fought," said my uncle. "If it were not for that bit of treachery Lindsay used on us with the spears, I think they would be the ones leaving the field of battle with us in pursuit of them."

"Aye," replied Gordon. "Even with that initial setback I think we killed many more of them than they did of us. It's a pity that they outnumbered us at the start."

"Their greater numbers won't matter so much now," my uncle replied. "We won't be falling for any more of their tricks and if we can get to the bridge over Aberbrothock Burn before they attack again, we'll be fine. We'll form a stout shield wall across the roadway and Lindsay will have to attack us head on. He won't be able to outflank us since the water is too deep to easily cross there. Even if some do manage to get across the burn, the woods are too thick in that area for any force to navigate through."

My uncle's words were reassuring and they made sense, however I still felt uneasy about the circumstances we were in. I estimated we had lost over a third of our force. In addition to the dead or badly injured, others had left the field to accompany wounded family members to safety. Although we had inflicted more causalities on Lindsay's force, they had more to lose. We couldn't win a battle of attrition, so I knew we had to stand firm at the Aberbrothock Bridge.

I was started out of my morose thoughts by shouts of "They're coming! They're coming!" and quickly turned to see what was happening. A large cloud of dust behind us gave evidence that Lindsay's force was on the move and heading in our direction. They were about a mile behind us and we still had about a mile to reach the bridge where we had decided to make our stand.

"Campbell, go back to the front and hurry the men along," Gordon said as he gently grabbed my arm and pushed me forward. "After you cross over the bridge, assign 20 men to guard each side in case Lindsay does try to outflank us. After you've gotten our flanks covered, come back to the bridge with your best men and we'll form our shield wall."

"I'll take care of it," I replied and quickly returned to the front of the line. The men were already moving faster under Duncan's urgings and we quickly covered the distance to the bridge.

After we had crossed over I quickly picked two groups of 20 men each and assigned them the job of making sure none of Lindsay's men attacked us from either side. I told them that if they saw any men coming through the woods they were to immediately attack them. If any of Lindsay's men did make it across the burn I knew we stood a better chance of repulsing them while they were still struggling through the woods than we would if they got through and were able to regroup.

After making sure everyone on our flanks knew what they were supposed to do, I went back to the bridge. I took Duncan and Malcome with me, along with a number of other men that I knew would acquit themselves well in a shield wall. James had joined us and asked to fight with us on the bridge. He insisted he was fit and able in spite of his wound so I allowed him to stay.

The rest of our force was already on the bridge and Gordon was quickly getting men into position for a shield wall. James and I were in the front row as was my uncle. We tried to persuade my uncle not to take such a dangerous job, but he insisted. Malcome and Duncan were in the second row directly behind us with their spears at the ready.

By the time our wall was formed, Lindsay and his forces were less than 50 yards from us. They stopped and were shouting insults at us, daring us to come and fight them, "like real men instead of cowering behind your shields."

We also shouted insults at them, and this standoff went on for over an hour with no side making any moves toward the other. There was now less than two hours of daylight left and Lindsay realized that if he wanted to fight he would have to make the first move.

I watched as Lindsay conferred with his lieutenants. After a brief conversation, his lieutenants returned to their men and their front ranks began moving towards us. Their front row consisted of men with shields and behind them were spearmen. As they moved slowly but inexorably towards us I saw some of Lindsay's men peel off from the main body and head towards the burn. I looked around and called to Gordon to warn him what was happening, but he and Sande had already seen and were taking some of our men from our reserves back to bolster our flank defenses.

I began to feel better about our chances. Even though we were outnumbered we were in a strong defensive position where Lindsay couldn't use his superior numbers to an advantage. I was also confident that our men were better fighters. Nearly all of the men that had been at our training camp were fighting on our side and the results of that training had been evident in those men I saw engaged in that days initial fighting.

Lindsay's group had now stopped about 10 yards in front of our lines. Both sides were screaming insults at the other and some of the men on Lindsay's side were throwing rocks and even a couple of spears were thrown our way. All of their missiles were easily blocked.

We had passed the word to our men to save their energy and not throw rocks or waste spears and I was happy to see that our men refrained from giving into the urge to hurl any missiles at Lindsay's forces. We kept ourselves under control, swatting away any rocks and spears thrown our way, and waited for the charge from Lindsay that we knew would be coming soon.

We didn't have long to wait. As soon as Lindsay realized his missile barrage was a waste of energy and materials, we heard a loud scream of, "Now! At them, lads! Kill them all!" With a great roar, Lindsay's force came rushing at us.

Our shields smashed together and both sides began pushing at the other in an attempt to force a break in the shield wall. I was again within inches of a foul smelling, spitting and cursing bearded individual who was shouting insults and telling me what a horrible fate awaited me. His breath reeked of alcohol and I could see his eyes were red and bloodshot.

My uncle, in what I think was a very wise move, had stopped the flow of ale to our men early the night before. Lindsay, on the other hand, had arrived on the battlefield with a wagon load of kegs. I saw his men getting drinks from that wagon before and after our initial battle at the west gate. Many times during our training Sande had stressed the importance of being sober in a fight. "Alcohol gives you courage," Sande would say, "but it's a false courage that won't last, and it makes you reckless and clumsy."

I noticed that many, if not most of Lindsay's men had the same bloodshot eyes as the one directly in front of me. Most of the men kept up a constant litany of cursing and swearing, but I remained silent. I saved my breath and waited for an opening to strike a blow against the enemy. Due to the close quarters, I kept my sword sheathed but I had my axe in hand as I waited for a chance to use it.

My axe was a thing of beauty, if you can describe a weapon designed for killing people in the most gruesome fashion in that manner. It had a round handle about half the thickness of a man's wrist made of oak. For added strength and grip, it had four strips of metal running up and down its length that ended at the head of the axe. The head itself was about six inches across and had a blade on one side and a hook on the other. At the very tip of the axe was a spear point about three inches long. It was a very sturdy weapon that was deadly in close quarters.

James was to my right and was armed with a short sword when an axe suddenly slammed into the top of my shield, pulling it down and out of position. James saw what was happening and quickly slashed his sword down onto the arm of the person wielding the axe. The pressure on the axe quickly fell away and I was able to get my shield back into position before the enemy was able to take advantage of the situation.

Spears from both sides were being thrust over and under the shields, hoping to strike the enemy. Axes and maces were being slammed into the shields, hoping to shatter them or pull them away.

A man to my left caught the head of a mace on the top of his shield. The mace had been aimed at his head and the full force of the mace was blocked by the shield. However, the mace still gave him a glancing blow on his helmet which staggered him and he could not maintain his place in the shield wall.

As he fell back the man behind him struggled to take his place. The enemy saw this weakness in our line and tried to force their wall through. With this sudden weakness and increased pressure from the enemy, our line began to bulge backwards slightly. I knew we had to restore our wall quickly or our shield wall would break completely.

"At them lads, we must push them back!" I yelled at those around me. One of Lindsay's men on my left had pushed himself into this bulge in our line and was now nearly even with me. I saw that he was trying to get his sword up to strike at me but I managed to get my axe up and stab the end of it at the man's face. The point of my axe entered his head just above his left ear and the man dropped like a rock. Simultaneously a spear flashed over my head from behind, striking another enemy in the shoulder just above the tip of his shield.

These two blows blunted the enemy's advance and we were able to restore the stability of our shield wall. We were once more back to a static line of sweating, cursing men that were trying to strike one another over or under the lines of shields. Both sides continued trying to push through the others defenses, but neither line budged an inch.

The sudden sound of yelling and screaming to my left told me that some of Lindsay's forces had managed to cross the burn and were engaged with our men in the woods. I knew that if Lindsay's men were able to break through our flank we were done for. I took comfort in knowing that Sande was with the men on our left flank and that if anyone could stop Lindsay's men he was the one to do it. I also knew that whatever happened over there was completely out of my control. There was nothing I could do except hope that Sande had the situation well in hand.

Our shield walls were still locked tightly together, but I began to sense that Lindsay's forces were beginning to weaken slightly. At first I thought it was wishful thinking, but then I began to realize that it was getting harder for them to maintain the formation of their shield wall. The large amounts of liquid courage they had ingested throughout the day was now sapping their strength. Inch by inch their shield wall was giving ground. Our men could sense this weakening and it made them push harder.

The break in their wall was sudden and unexpected when it happened. One of our spears found its mark in the face of one of Lindsay's men. At the same time the man next to him had his shield pulled out of his hand by a well-placed chop of an axe and his now unprotected chest and abdomen was quickly pierced by a sword as well as a spear.

The sudden, complete loss of two of their men in the same spot caused their weakening shield wall to break completely, and with great cheers and yells we pushed through the gap in their line to begin the slaughter. For the second time that day we had broken Lindsay's shield wall and were inflicting terrible damage on his men. Although Lindsay himself could be heard exhorting his men to reform a new shield wall and stand firm, they could not stand up to our onslaught.

Duncan was next to me now and was using his spear with devastating precision. He thrust his spear through the chest of one man, and then pulled his weapon free by kicking the dying person backwards with his foot. As the point of the spear came out, along with great spouts of the man's blood, another of Lindsay's men raised his sword to strike Duncan. Duncan easily evaded the man's sword and then quickly swung the butt of the spear into the man's head who fell senseless to the ground. Without any pause in his motion, he then brought the head of the spear down viciously at a third man, slicing him open from his right shoulder to his left hip, spilling his blood and intestines on the ground.

It quickly became difficult to maintain our footing on the slick gore covered ground. A man raised his sword to strike at me but his feet slipped out from under him before he could bring his sword down and he fell backwards onto the ground. Even lying on his back he tried to swing his sword at my legs and I had to jump back quickly to avoid the arc as I shoved my own sword through his heart.

Malcome was engaged with another of Lindsay's men. They were exchanging fierce sword blows that were landing on each other's shields when Malcome also slipped and fell. As his enemy raised his sword to strike Malcome, I was able to quickly thrust my sword between the man's ribs. The man then gave out a howl of pain and dropped his weapon before collapsing next to Malcome.

James was also in the thick of the fighting. I saw him bring his sword down on the back of the neck of one of Lindsay's men. The poor fellow had slipped and fallen forward and was down on his hands and knees. James's sword neatly severed his head and the resulting gush of red liquid added more gore to the blood soaked ground.

Our men were taking a terrible toll on Lindsay's forces. They were now falling back rapidly, unable to defend themselves or regroup. I think we would have completely routed Lindsay's forces except the same thing that happened at the abbey earlier that day now happened at the bridge. The fighting and yelling that we had heard earlier off to our left was now louder and more intense and was now directly behind us.

A large number of Lindsay's men had managed to get across the burn, pushing the men back we had positioned to defend our flanks, and were now attacking at our rear. Even though we now were on the bridge with Lindsay's forces at either end our position was not as dire as it might seem. With the carnage we had inflicted on Lindsay's forces when we had twice broken their shield walls that day, their forces, although still more numerous than ours, were now not as great as they had been. The bridge itself afforded us protection in that any superior numbers that Lindsay did still retain could not be brought to any great advantage due to the confines of the bridge.

At any rate we still more than held our own against Lindsay's forces, although the casualties on both sides were high. In the end, the days fighting ceased not because one side was overwhelmed or left the field, but simply because both sides were exhausted and nightfall made it difficult to carry on the struggle.

Lindsay himself was the one to suggest a truce, shouting to make himself heard over the din of battle. In fact though, the fighting was starting to abate of its own accord, darkness and exhaustion taking the eagerness to fight away from both sides.

Gordon quickly accepted Lindsay's offer of a truce. We moved to one side of the bridge and allowed those Lindsay men that had crossed the burn to cross over the bridge unmolested, carrying their dead and wounded. We then set about the grim task of caring for our injured and gathering the bodies of our dead. The Battle of Arbroath was at an end.

Chapter 28

It's hard to describe the feelings I had after the battle. I felt relief that the battle was over and I had survived. I also felt a great deal of satisfaction knowing that I had acquitted myself at least reasonably well. The feelings of relief and satisfaction combined to produce an incredibly strong sense of well-being and happiness. I've had the same feeling after other battles but not to the extent I felt after this one. It was something close to euphoria. Unfortunately the happy feeling was not to last for long.

As I was walking off the bridge I saw the large shape of Duncan approaching me through the gathering dusk. "Campbeel, aam afraid ah hae bad bark fur ye. It's yer uncle, he's hurt bad."

"Where is he?" I asked.

"Ower thaur by th' lights. Aam sorry Campbeel, but he's nae

doin' weel at aw." Duncan answered, pointing to a group of men holding torches.

I quickly made my way towards the group of men that were illuminated by the torchlight. They were standing in a circle looking down at something or someone on the ground. I quickly pushed my way through and saw to my shock and dismay that the figure on the ground was my uncle.

He had suffered a grievous wound to his abdomen and his blood had saturated his clothing and was seeping onto the ground. I quickly knelt beside him, taking his hand and softly called his name. His eyes were closed when I first saw him but when he heard his name he opened his eyes. He looked at me and I said, "Uncle, we need to get that wound treated. We need you to get better."

My uncle smiled slightly and squeezed my hand as he said, "Ah laddie, I'm sorry but I won't be getting better, we both know that." I could feel the tears welling in my eyes as he continued. "Please make sure Janet and young Alexander are taken care of, and do all you can to keep Lindsay's hands off Inverquharity."

"I will, Uncle; I'll make sure they're well cared for," I replied.

"I know you will, Campbell, and knowing that helps me to rest easy." With that said, my uncle closed his eyes again and his grip on my hand relaxed. I thought he had given up the ghost at that moment but then I saw that he still drew breath, although it was now coming in a ragged fashion.

"We must get my uncle out of this damp and to a place of warmth," I said to the crowd gathered about.

"There is a church just down the road in the town of Kinnell," someone in the crowd said.

"Let's get him there as quickly as possible," I replied. My uncle was quickly hoisted aloft by several willing hands and we started down the road to the church. We carried several other wounded with us and we also took the remains of Forbes of Pitsligo. His standing in society dictated his body being singled out for special treatment.

A couple dozen of our comrade's volunteered to stay behind and undertake the unpleasant job of burying our dead. Our fallen were all interred in a number of mass graves. Those graves later had cairns erected over them that I understand are still there to this day.

Upon arriving in Kinnell, we located the priest who told us we were welcome to use the church for the care of our wounded. He also gave us permission to use the building next to the church that had been the manse, but was now unoccupied. Since the old manse had a fireplace, we decided to put the wounded there. Most of our uninjured men had left for their homes, but those of us who stayed spent the night in the church.

We quickly started a fire which took the night's chill off and we made my uncle and the rest of the wounded as comfortable as possible. Some of the village women came with food and water and also strips of linen to bandage wounds.

The priest was a kindly older man who knew my uncle. He was visibly shaken when he saw how badly my uncle was injured. The priest, whose name was Father Henry Chepman, gave my uncle and two other badly wounded men, the last rites.

As the night progressed, Uncle Alexander's breathing was more shallow and ragged. He became unresponsive and shortly after midnight he passed away. We wrapped his body for burial and I got a few hours of sleep before the first rays of the morning sun began to illuminate the old manse.

In the morning, we buried Forbes along with another man that had passed during the night. We interred them in the meadow next to the church, known as Threap Meadow, and erected cairns over the graves. We were going to bury my uncle in the same fashion but the priest, who evidently had a high regard for my uncle, insisted that he be buried in the aisle of the church.

I was very grateful for the honor that Father Chepman bestowed upon Uncle Alexander as were the rest of us there. To this day I understand that this part of the church is known as the Ogilvy aisle and there is even an inscription that was placed on the aisle that reads: "While griss grows green and water rins clear, let nane but Oglivys lie here."[1]

James had gone home after the wounded had been made secure. He had wanted to stay the night but he was in a lot of pain from the wound to his face. I told him we had lots of help and he would recover faster at home. He reluctantly left shortly after midnight in the company of two other slightly wounded men that lived near him.

Duncan and Malcome, along with Gordon and Sande, had

---

1   *pg 66 of "History of Arbroath"*

stayed the night and I was thankful that that they did. After the burials the five of us discussed what our next course of action should be.

"Dae ye hink we can gang back haem noo ur shoods we stick aroond tae caur fur uir woonded?" Malcome inquired.

"Our lads are in good hands," Gordon responded. "No one, not even Lindsay himself would dare raise a hand against them while they're under the protection of mother church. They'll be well taken care of here until they're mended. Furthermore," Gordon continued with a worried expression, "it's imperative we get home to our families as soon as possible. I'm afraid with the death of Alexander Ogilvy and David Lindsay, combined with the newest Earl of Crawford's superior numbers, there will be no way to restrain Lindsay. I'm afraid that he and his followers will burn our homes and castles, plunder our property and commit unspeakable acts against our vassals and families."

My blood ran cold when I heard Gordon's warnings. "Surely not even Lindsay would be that monstrous" I asked.

"I'm afraid he will be that monstrous," Gordon replied. "Lindsay wants revenge and he also wants to make sure that the population will be too afraid to rise up against him again. He's quite capable of that and worse. Actually, from the point of view of someone that has no morals or restraints, it makes perfect sense to do that."

"Then we should leave immediately," I said, and everyone was in agreement with that. The three of us said our goodbyes to Gordon and Sande and embraced them before they headed north. The three of us then started on the long trek back to our homes.

Setting out on foot towards Arbroath, we discussed what would be the safest route to take back. Initially we thought that bypassing Arbroath entirely would be the safest way but we decided against that. That would have added miles to an already long journey and we hoped that we still had horses quartered in the abbey. We also realized that there was just as good a chance of running into Lindsay's men in the countryside as there was in Arbroath and at least in town if we had a problem there might be friends that could come to our aid.

It turned out we needn't had worried. Arbroath was all but deserted. The few people we did encounter as we entered the town quickly disappeared out of sight. Surprisingly, there were few signs of the battle that had taken place there just the day before. There were a few spots of dried blood on the ground here and there and we saw an occasional broken weapon, but not as much as I had anticipated we would find.

We made our way to the abbey and banged on the door. A voice from the other side asked who we were and what our business was. We explained who we were and inquired about our horses. The voice asked us to wait a moment while he consulted the abbot. Within a short while, the door began to open and Abbot Walter himself was there to greet us.

"Campbell, thank God the three of you, at least, are alive!" the abbot exclaimed. "Is it true what they're saying about your uncle? Is he truly dead?"

"I'm afraid so Father," I replied. "He fought bravely but suffered a grievous wound during the fighting that he could not recover from. He passed this morning, just after midnight. The priest at the church in Kinnell, Father Chepman, afforded him the honor of being buried in the church aisle. We interred him there this morning."

The abbot crossed himself before replying "It was good of Father Chepman to have done that. Your uncle was a good man and he will be sorely missed." In a lower voice, almost as if he were talking to himself, the abbot continued, "With the death of Alexander and Lindsay's father now, there is no one to control the new Earl of Crawford." Changing his tone the abbot then said, "I suppose you boys have come for your horses. Some of Lindsay's men came to get them, but we refused them entrance. At first I was afraid they were going to knock the gate down and take them but they didn't. Perhaps that means they at least have some respect for the church."

"Ur mebbe they jist didne want tae tak' th' time. Those rogues' kent thaur waur easier targets around." Malcome replied. His comment gave me a sick feeling in my stomach. I knew those easier targets would be our homes and families.

"I hope you're wrong, Malcome," the abbot replied. "Sadly however, you're probably right. But come; have a bite to eat and then I'll take you to your horses. I know you're anxious to be on the road."

We gratefully wolfed down a late breakfast of porridge and dried mutton that the monks provided for us and then let the abbot take us to our horses. We quickly saddled our mounts and left the abbey at a swift pace, alternating between a slow gallop and then trots to give the horses a rest.

We hadn't gone far when we saw the first plumes of smoke on the horizon. "Swatch thaur!" Duncan said with a note of alarm in his voice as he pointed towards the distant columns of smoke. We stopped our horses for a few seconds, staring at the ominous black and grey clouds that were rising in the sky. The sick feeling in my stomach I had had earlier came back, only much worse.

Without another word, we all spurred our horses to a gallop. The uneasiness we had felt earlier was now replaced by the certainties and fear that something was terribly wrong.

We pushed our horses as fast and as hard as we could until we came to the lane that led to Malcome's farm. As soon as we turned into the lane, which was about a mile from the barns and dwellings, Malcome's ancestral home, we could see flames leaping into the air and smell the awful sickening odor of burning flesh. We slowed our horses to a walk. We knew whatever sights we were going to see would not be good, but we weren't prepared for the utter devastation that we saw.

Malcome's home, a tower castle that had been built over 200 years before, was in ruins. Flames were still showing in the castle as timbers continued to burn. The structure itself was beginning to collapse as the fire ate away at the supports and weakened the mortar that had held the stones together.

All the structures on his family's farm were destroyed. The barn and animals inside had been incinerated. A few animals had been able to escape the fire but they had been butchered as soon as they had run out and their bodies lay on the ground where they had fallen.

The homes where the farm workers had lived had also been torched and the remains were either smoldering or still in flames. There seemed to not be any structure to small or unimportant to escape the fury of Lindsay's wrath.

The worse destruction however were the human lives that had been taken. The prostrate forms of four people lay among the ruins of what had once been a prosperous estate. The bodies of an elderly couple lay not far from the ruins of what must have been their home. A pitchfork still grasped in the man's hands gave evidence that he had tried to fight off the attackers.

Closer to the remains of the castle were the bodies of a young boy, barely into his teens, and an older man. These were the remains of Malcome's father and his youngest brother.

Malcome made no sound as he slowly walked towards the bodies. First Malcome went and knelt by his brother. He tenderly smoothed the hair back off his forehead before rising and walking over to his father. He grasped the lifeless man's hand as he knelt by the remains. The crackling and burning of the fires nearly drowned out the sounds of Malcome quietly sobbing.

Chapter 29

Seeing the terrible destruction at Malcome's home increased my fear and worry about my own family. I struggled to control my urge to gallop as fast as I could to Inverquharity. I knew that my friends needed me as much as I needed them and I also knew that anything we might encounter would be better faced together.

After a few minutes Malcome recovered somewhat and the three of us proceeded to give the remains a hurried burial. It was now shortly after noon. We knew we had two more stops before we could rest for the day so we got back on the road towards Duncan's farm as quickly as we could.

Malcome's place was less than two miles from Duncan's and as soon as we got back on the main road we saw spirals of smoke rising in the air over Duncan's homestead. We pushed our horses as fast as we could even though we knew that the sights we would see when we reached our destination would not be pleasant.

Our expectations were justified. The devastation we witnessed at Duncan's farm was worse than where we had just left. In addition to the complete burning and destruction of all the structures there were more than a dozen bodies lying about.

Two of the women showed evidence of being sexually violated. One of them looked to be a child barely into her teens. Both lay on their backs with their skirts pulled up to their necks and their legs were in that unnatural oval shape that spoke of sexual violence. Both had their necks slit.

The other bodies lay where they had fallen. The horrendous stab and slashing wounds that were visible through the dried blood on the remains was evidence of the horrible violence these people had been subject to.

Duncan had an advantage over Malcome in that at least his immediate family was not among the slain. His parents were long since deceased and his siblings were scattered throughout Scotland and England. The lack of family killed, however, didn't lessen the outrage we all felt at these innocent people that had been slain.

As we walked through this scene of violence we happened across two bodies that we had not seen before. They were lying on their backs on the far side of a wagon that had been turned on its side. These two bore no signs of violence and had swords strapped to their waists. We quickly realized that these were not victims of the violence but rather were two of the perpetrators. They had obtained jugs of whisky from one of the storehouses and had drunk themselves to a state of insensibility. Their comrades were probably not able to rouse them and so had left them to sober up on their own.

We quickly removed their swords and an axe and knife we found under their cloaks. William fetched a bucket of water from a horse watering trough and splashed the ice cold contents on the sleeping men.

"Its time fur ye fellows tae wake up an' answer a puckle of questions," Duncan said in a calm voice that showed no emotion. Although he appeared calm on the outside I knew that a violent rage was inside Duncan, as it was for all three of us.

When the cold water struck them the two awoke with a start and went for their swords but only found empty scabbards. We had our own swords at their throats. The sight of the three of us staring down at them, with weapons drawn, put fear in their hearts that showed clearly on their faces.

We put our swords under their chins and by bringing the sword tips up against their chins forced them to their feet. We pushed them roughly backwards until their backs were against the bottom of the overturned wagon. We then lashed both their hands, spread-eagled; to what was now the top of the wagon.

"Ye cannae treat us lik thes. We're haur oan behalf ay th' justicar ay Angus. Ye mus free us immeaditly," the taller of the two said with a heavy highland brough.

"Haud yer weesht ye worthless son ay a huir. Ye say anither

wuid afair ah teel ee tae, I weel cut yer tongue ot," Duncan answered him harshly at the same time as he punched him full in the mouth, breaking his teeth and splitting his lips.

As the now chastened man spit blood and teeth between his bleeding lips we heard a sound coming from the other side of the wagon. Looking in the direction the sound was coming from we saw a group of about 15 people, women and some children, coming out of the woods and heading in our direction.

Many in their group ran to where they saw loved ones lying prostrate on the ground, and began to wail and cry over the lifeless bodies. A few of the others came to where we were holding our prisoners.

"The monsters! The bloody monsters! They killed us for no reason. We told them they could take anything they wanted but they killed us anyway!" one woman with long disheveled hair and tears streaming down her face shouted at us as she came close.

"Calm yerself, Jessie. We'll git th' bastards 'at did thes, ah pledge ee," Duncan answered the women as he held her tightly in his arms. She clung to him and sobbed uncontrollably against him.

"Those two were part of the group that attacked us," another women, whose name we found out later was Margaret, stated as she motioned toward the men we had tied against the wagon. "They would have killed us all if some of us hadn't managed to get into the woods." Continuing on she said, "We saw you as you rode up. At first we thought you were part of Lindsay's group, come back to cause more harm, but then we recognized Duncan. Thank the Lord it's you and not more of those pigs." She spat on the ground for emphasis as she finished.

At this point we heard another woman screaming, "Look what they've done! Look what they've done to me poor Thebe!" As she was screaming she was walking towards us, holding the body of the young girl that had been raped and murdered.

Malcome and I went to try and help her but she wouldn't let anyone touch the body of her daughter. She dragged and carried the body until she stood directly in front of the taller prisoner with the bloody mouth.

She spat directly into his face and shouted, "He's the one. He's the one that grabbed my Thebe and threw her on the ground. I seen everything from the woods. I tried to run to her but the others grabbed me and wouldn't let me go. He's also the one who slit her throat after they were done with her. I want to kill him! I want to kill him with my bare hands!"

Malcome took her and her lifeless daughter in his arms and she allowed him to lead her away from the wagon and let her daughter slide gently to the ground. However as soon as her daughter's body was out of her arms she ran back to the prisoner and attacked him. She used her hands to claw at his eyes and she kicked and kneed him until Malcome was again able to grab her and again lead her away as she sobbed and cried hysterically.

"What do you intend to do with those two?" Margaret asked me as more of the survivors of the attack walked up to us.

"I have no idea," I replied. "There is no justice in Angus anymore with Lindsay having taken over."

"Then leave them here. We will deal with them in an appropriate fashion. We will see they receive the justice they deserve," she responded in a very calm, almost detached voice.

I looked at the women now gathered around and saw many nodding their heads in agreement at what Margaret had suggested. "Aye, leave them with us," one of them said. "We'll take care of them," another said as they all nodded their heads in agreement.

Duncan and Malcome, having been able to calm the two distraught women enough to leave them, had now joined our group. "Did you hear what the women have suggested?" I asked them.

"Aye," they both said in unison.

"What do you think we should do then?"

"We shoods dae whit these braw lasses want. Am sure those twa will be in guid hans if we lae them wi' th' kimers," Malcome answered me.

Duncan nodded his head to show he was in agreement so I turned to Margaret and said, "Very well, the prisoners are yours to do what you will with them. We'll help you bury your dead and then well be on our way."

"That's very kind of you but we can bury them on our own. Is nae bother. I know you have your own family to look after. You should go to them without further delay," she responded.

I knew Margaret was right so Malcome and I said our good-byes. Duncan wanted to stay but Margaret and the others convinced him he should accompany us so he also said good-bye and the three of us went to where we had tied our horses.

It wasn't too long after we had mounted our horses to begin the trip to Inverquharity that we heard the first screams of horror and pain coming from the direction of where we had tied our prisoners.

As we rode past the wagon the women that had lost her daughter came around the side. She had a maniacal smile on her face and her linen dress was splattered with blood. She had her hands lifted above her head and was doing a little dance. She was holding something in each hand.

She came close to us as we rode by and said, "Look! Look at the nice present I have for Lindsay when I see him again." She opened her hands enough for us to see what she held. Her right hand held a man's penis and testicles and her left hand held a neatly gouged out eyeball.

We continued on our way, anxious to be gone from such a place of horror. The sights we had seen made me even more apprehensive about what we would see when we reached Inverquharity.

"Those tois willnae be alife fur lang," Duncan commented.

"They'll probably be alive a lot longer than they want to be at this moment," I replied.

The screams of pain and anguish followed us as we turned onto the road to Inverquharity.

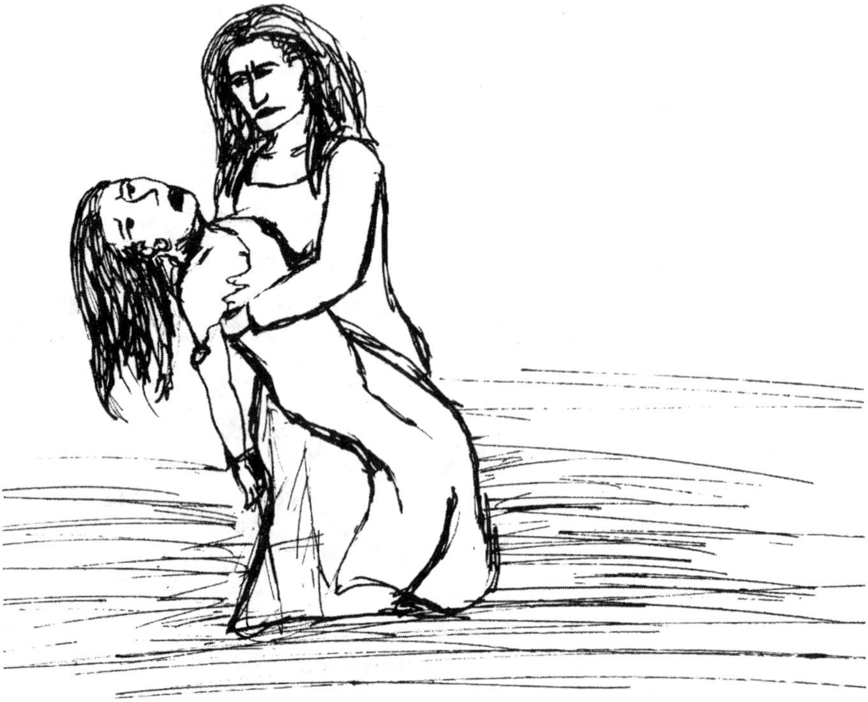

Chapter 30

We rode towards Inverquharity as fast as we could push our horses and, as with the other farms; we could see telltale spires of smoke over where I knew my home should be. However, I noticed that these smoke spirals were not as numerous or dense. I didn't know why this was so but I know I didn't have time to dwell on it. The terrible sense of forbidding I had had all day was only getting worse and the only thoughts I had were that I had to get home as fast as I could.

The distance from Duncan's home to Inverquharity was only three miles but it seemed unending, so great was my worry and fear for Ellene and my other family members.

As we finally drew near to Inverquharity I turned my horse into the lane leading to the castle at a full gallop. Pulling into the courtyard I noticed that the annex where I lived with my family had been destroyed and burned but the main part of the castle was still standing untouched.

I pulled my horse to a halt and dismounted with Duncan and Malcome close behind me. There was no sign of Lindsey's men but we still felt a sense of foreboding as we began to walk about the grounds and we kept our hands on the pommels of our swords.

Other than the destruction of the annex there didn't appear to be any other damage done to the farm. The barns and outbuildings were still intact with the animals still in their pens. The homes of the tenant farmers were untouched and the wagons and farm implements undamaged. However, there was an eerie silence about the place and there were no sign of any of the inhabitants.

We went up to the castle and was about to knock on the door when we heard a voice behind us.

"Psst, Campbell, it's me, Thom," and we turned around to see our servant beckoning to us from a grove of trees.

We walked over to where Thom was standing. In a low voice, as if he was afraid of being heard he began, "You're not safe here, none of you." Turning to me he continued, "Your uncle Thomas has given an oath to support Lindsay, part of that oath was to assist in helping in any way he can to apprehend you and your two friends. It appears that Lindsay has declared you three to be wanted men and has put a price on all your heads."

"What has happened to Ellene, and my mother and sister?" I frantically asked, the fear I felt affecting the sound of my voice.

Thom looked apprehensive and was silent for a few seconds. Then he swallowed hard and said. "Lindsey took them all, Campbell. He said he's holding them until you're apprehended or turn yourself in. I'm sorry, Campbell, there was nothing I or anyone could do to stop them, there were too many of them."

I felt like I had been kicked in the stomach. My knees felt weak and I had trouble standing. Composing myself I asked, "Where did he take them to?"

"I don't know," Thom replied. "But my guess would be Glamis Castle. Lindsey is close friends with the Douglas's."

"Wa did they only destroy th' annex an leave th lae, th' castle an' groonds, untouched?" Duncan asked.

"They were going to put the whole place to the torch," Thom replied, "but Lindsey agreed to spare most of Inverquharity if Thomas swore an oath of allegiance to him. However, even with the oath Lindsay insisted that the annex be destroyed, since that was Campbell's home. According to Lindsay, since some Ogilvy's were disloyal, then some of Inverquharity must be destroyed."

"So my uncle Thomas has turned traitor and allowed my wife and family to be taken hostage," I said as my fear and worry began to be joined by a growing rage. "I should go in there now and cut Thomas's black heart out of his chest."

"Don't be too hard on your uncle, Campbell" Thom replied. "If Thomas had not given his oath to Lindsay this entire place would be a smoking ruin now and we'd all be dead."

Malcome laid his hand on my shoulder as he said in a reassuring voice "Ah ken yoo're woriat abit yer fowk campbeel but at leest they're alife an' we'll dae whatever we hae tae dae tae rescue em."

"Och aye, we'll gie them back campbeel, we willnae rest until we dae" Duncan joined in.

I felt somewhat better by their reassuring words and was grateful to have two such close friends that I knew I could depend on.

"I don't suppose there's anything we can do here then is there?" I asked Thom, knowing full well the answer before I asked the question.

"Not a thing. The best the three of you can do right now is to get yourselves to a place of safety," Thon replied. "And Campbell, I hope your family is safe and well and that you'll be able to rescue them. Before you go, follow me back to my quarters. You and your horses both look like you could use a good meal."

We gratefully followed Thom to a small wooden structure he and his wife, Besse, had fled to when Lindsey and his cohorts arrived. Besse fed the three of us and Thom took care of the feeding of our horses. After we had eaten Thom and his wife insisted on giving us ample provisions to take with us even though I know they had barely enough for themselves.

It was dark by the time we had gotten back on the road. None of us knew exactly where we were going but we all knew we needed to leave Angus as quickly as possible. We needed a safe place to rest and regroup and make plans to rescue my family.

We rode slowly along in silence, back the way we had come. I didn't know where I was going or if I would ever see Ellene and my mother and sister alive again. One thing I did know was that somehow, somewhere, I would meet up with Lindsey again and that I would kill him.

A light cold rain had begun to fall and we wrapped our cloaks tightly about us. I was grateful for the cold and the rain. The cold helped to numb the feelings of despair I felt and the rain hid the tears that streamed down my cheeks whenever I thought of Ellene.

Historical Note

Not much has been written about the Battle of Arbroath. Most historians, if they mention it at all, dismiss it as an example of feudal violence between clans that was all too prevalent in those days. However the Battle of Arbroath was much more than a simple feud between clans. It was actually part of the ongoing power struggle between the powerful house of Clan Douglas and the Scottish kingdom which was controlled by the royal house of Stuart.

The wars with England had weakened the authority of the Crown. The Scottish king during this time period, James II, was only a child of six when he became the Monarch. The age of the king, along with the weakened authority of the Monarchy, made for a society that was unstable with a great deal of unlawfulness. It was during this period of uncertainty and upheaval that the Douglas's became nearly as powerful as the Crown.

It was against this background that two powerful clans in the county of Angus, Clan Lindsay and Clan Ogilvy became bitter enemies over the appointment of Alexander Ogilvy to the position of Justicar. The position of Justicar, or Bailie of regality, gave the person who held that office the authority to dispense law and justice as well as to levy and collect taxes throughout the county. It was a very powerful as well as lucrative position.

I tried to make this novel as historically accurate as possible. Although Campbell Ogilvy and his friends were fictitious, most of the other major characters in this book were real people. Alexander Lindsay and his father David Lindsay were, respectively, the Third and Fourth Earls of Crawford. Historical accounts of Alexander Lindsay paint him as a fierce and lawless individual although I doubt he was as bad a person as I've made him appear, nor I doubt that his father, David, was as good an individual as he is in this book. (In fact at the time of his death, David Lindsay had been excommunicated from the church by James Kennedy, arch-bishop of St Andrews).

The start of the Battle of Arbroath happened as depicted in this novel. David Lindsay was struck down by a spear thrown by one of the Ogilvy supporters as he rode between the two armies in a valiant, but vain attempt to prevent the fighting.

Alexander Ogilvy and his brothers Walter and Thomas were part of the prominent Ogilvy clan during this time. Sir Alexander Seton of Gordon, Earl of Huntly, was a very powerful Scottish nobleman that was referred to as the "Cock of the North". Sir Gordon had his first marriage annulled so he could marry another woman, effectively disinheriting his child from that first marriage. That child was a son, also with the given name of Alexander, who I referred to in this book as Sande.

James Douglas and his son, William Douglas were, respectively, the Seventh and Eighth Earl of Douglas. William was a cousin of the Sixth Earl of Douglas, who, along with his brother, were murdered at the Black Dinner in 1440.

The Battle of Arbroath is reported to have started at the west gate of Arbroath Abbey and evolved into a running battle that finally ended at the Loan of the Leys, about three miles from the abbey.

The loss of life on both sides was quite substantial but the death of Alexander Ogilvy along with Alexander Lindsay's father made Lindsay the victor of the battle since he now had no one to oppose or control him. The aftermath of the battle saw a great deal of reprisals and atrocities committed against the Ogilvy's and their supporters.

The power struggle between Clan Douglas and the Scottish Crown continued for a number of years and two more battles before being settled at the Battle of Arkinholm in 1455.

I hope you enjoyed reading about Campbell Ogilvy's exploits in this book and hope you continue to follow Campbell through the battle of Brechin and then through the Battle of Arkinholm.

Bibliography

Buchanan, George. *The History of Scotland, Volume 2*. 1827

Brown, Jennifer M. ed. *Scottish Society in the Fifteenth Century*. London: Arnold. 1977

Cowan, Edward J. and Henderson, Lizanne ed. *A History of Everyday Life in Medieval Scotland, 1000 to 1600*. Edinburgh: Edinburgh University Press. 1988

Gies, Frances & Joseph. *Life in a Medieval Village*. New York: Harper Collins. 1991

Hay, George. *History of Arbroath to the present time*. Second edition. T Buncle & co. 1899

Mackay, James ed. *Pocket Scottish History*. Bath: Parragon. 2002

Newman, Paul B. *Daily Life in the Middle Ages*. London: McFarland & Company. 2001

Scott, Michael. *Scottish Wild Flowers*. Edinburgh: West Newington House. 2012

Warrack, Alexander. *Scots Dialect Dictionary*. New Lanark: Waverley. 2000